D1368111

Also by Milton Fisher

Intuition: How to Use It for
Success and Happiness

How to Make Big Money in the
Over-the-Counter Market

Haven't You Been Single Long Enough?

A Practical Guide for Men or Women Who Want to Get Married

by

Milton Fisher

Wildcat Publishing Company, Inc.

Haven't You Been Single Long Enough?

Wildcat Publishing Company, Inc.
Box 366
Green Farms, Ct. 06436

First Edition

Book designed by Irwin Wolf

Jacket designed by William Gregory

Library of Congress Cataloging-in-Publication Data

Fisher, Milton
    Haven't you been single long enough? : a practical guide for
men or women who want to get married / by Milton Fisher.
        p.   cm.
    ISBN 0-941968-03-0
    1. Mate selection. 2. Dating (Social customs) 3. Single people.
I. Title.
HQ801.F57 1992   91-41102
646.7'7—dc20   CIP

*This book is dedicated
with affection and gratitude to
my editor, coach, guide, cheerleader, backseat driver,
and wife,
Carol Plaine Fisher*

Contents

Introduction

Are you single? If you are, this book was written especially for you. What I have to share with you is rather personal and would best be discussed as friends over lunch. But since that ideal setting is not possible this book will have to do.

By profession, I'm a lawyer and investment banker. By avocation, a teacher and writer. However, my overriding passion is matchmaking! As a marriage activist, I have arranged hundreds of introductions and blind dates, and started scores of romances and many, many relationships. Twenty-nine have resulted in lasting marriages—not a single divorce!

This didn't happen by magic. There were thousands of one-on-one searching discussions with lonely men and women of all ages from every walk of life. This book contains the best of the insights and experiences we shared.

Some of the things you will read here you already know, some you may think obvious and just haven't thought of yet, but somewhere in this book you will find an idea or two that could change your life for the better.

The advice is for men and women in their twenties, thirties, forties—all the way up to seventy and beyond—who are single but still have an appetite for life. Maybe you are divorced, widowed, or just missed the brass ring on the last go-around. Whatever the reason you are single today, you don't have to be single any longer than you want to be.

Probably the most important step you will take in your life is marriage. So much of your future happiness and fulfillment is rooted in that single step. So many people have already experienced the adventure you face in finding a lifelong partner. Some of their stories will make your path a little smoother.

This book was inspired by the hundreds of men and women who were generous enough to share experiences and relevant chapters of their lives. Much of what we learn as we make our way through life is garnered from our own experiences, but most comes from the experience of others and I thank them.

Special thanks go to my daughter, Dr. Shelley Fisher Fishkin, for her encouragement, approval, and enthusiasm from the beginning, and to Lynne Lumsden and Cynthia Keyworth for their editorial guidance.

Names, places, and descriptions have been changed to protect the privacy of individuals, but all anecdotes and characters in this book are rooted in truth. Every tale contains a lesson and some guidance for the receptive mind.

A lifetime of matchmaking has given me a ringside seat for observing how people come together, learn to love one another, and then get married. I'd like to share what I've learned with you.

Haven't You Been Single Long Enough?

1

Hooray for Marriage!

Hooray for marriage! is what this book is all about. I truly believe that most people should be married. All of us can thrive on the caring, committed relationship that a marriage brings. We need a best friend to share our life. We need someone we can love who in turn will love us, someone who is warm, compassionate, and understanding and who will appreciate those loving qualities in us. The need to share love and life is in all of us, regardless of who we are.

Marriage offers more than the delights of being a couple. If you are fortunate, marriage fosters a joining of families and friends. A warm, close extended family of relatives and friends enriches and expands the quality of life. Yes, it brings responsibilities and obligations, but it also offers love and support and a network of people interested in your welfare.

What a tragedy if you were to miss all of this because you gave up looking or because you mistakenly believed that marriage was not meant for you.

Most people want to get married; they dream about it, look forward to it, and are comforted by the belief that it will come to them in time. Alas, many singles are like a car stuck in a snowdrift—spinning their wheels, going nowhere—destined for a long winter night.

Nobody ever learned to ski from reading a book or watching a training film. Sooner or later you must put on the skis and get out on the slopes. No one can teach you anything. You teach yourself; it's all self-revelation and personal insight. The "teacher" only acts as a guide, coach, or cheerleader.

Let's carry the analogy of skiing a bit further. Once you've taught yourself to ski and you're about to try skiing down a new slope, it's mighty helpful if someone coaches you about what to watch out for, how to avoid traps, and what to do when you reach a cluster of trees. It's also comforting to hear your coach say, "You can do it!"

The great adventure of marriage begins with just a single step, yet so many people can't take that first step! A timely nudge in the right direction is the job of the matchmaker. And that's what this book is for: to give you a timely nudge with some friendly guidance and practical insights. With just a little coaching, you'll be off on your own and have an exhilarating time.

Congratulations. You're at the start of a great adventure. The fact that you're reading this book means that you're now willing to change both yourself and your present scenario. You're willing to get involved in activities in which you will meet new people, to go on blind dates, and to get to know old and new friends on another, deeper level. Most importantly, you're willing to take chances, be tolerant of others, practice being loving and nurturing, and acquire some self-knowledge.

These skills, after all, don't apply to spouse hunting alone. Risk taking and change are what an interesting life is all about.

What stops people from finding the right marriage partner? If you answered "chemistry," then this book is definitely for you! Too many people dream of a lifelong love affair on the basis of instant "chemistry"— by which they usually mean sexual attraction. They also set such rigid standards and criteria that no Prince or Princess Charming could ever fulfill them. They're looking for an idealized "one-and-only," an image built up in their minds from thousands of sources—movies, television, books, advertisements and commercials, and input from mothers, fathers, sisters, brothers, friends, heroes, and rogues. They build an image of perfection that never was and never will be, measuring every date against this paragon. They keep searching for this imaginary lover and thus block the chance to find a *real* one-and-only.

Once I decide to set up a blind date, I'm usually overwhelmed with instructions on "essential" criteria: "Remember, I hate short men." "I can't stand career women." "I dislike snobs." "I need someone I can look up to." "I've got to have someone wholesome like my mom or my dad." "Someone good-looking." "Elegant." "Intellectual." "Sexy." "Cultured." And so on and so forth. (If they demand "rich," I quietly put them in the reject file. Let them work with an IRS agent!)

I pay little attention to these frenzied specifications because I've learned an important secret over the years. The truth is we really don't know for sure what we want. The "appetite comes with eating." Your one-and-only can only be homegrown.

Here's what I mean. I once teased my first wife in the early years of our marriage by saying, "You know, there were probably dozens of women out there that I could have been happily married to." Before she exploded, I added, "And probably twice as many men who could have been happy with you! But now I'm ruined. You are my one-and-only and I can't conceive of anyone I'd rather share my life with. You know, I hardly knew you when we got married. I didn't know what I was getting. I didn't know what marriage was all about."

Marriage itself creates the one-and-only relationship. That's the wonder and the joy of it. All of the dating, the engagement, the wedding itself, later the joint plans, the compromises, the conclusions, the friends and relations you share, the sex, the kids, the risks and the rewards—all of these create a treasury of experience and memories nobody in the world shares with you but your spouse, who becomes your home-grown one-and-only.

Becoming a Matchmaker

My zest for matchmaking came about by accident when I was a happy-go-lucky college student. As a joke, I told my friend Fred that a gorgeous girl in English 101 had a crush on him. Fred turned the tables on me and said he'd like to meet her. Now I had to come up with the girl! There were fourteen in the English class; I studied them carefully. Which one would he like? Which one might like him? Who had the right personality and the looks?

Finally, I made a choice and told her that I had a friend who was dying to meet her. She was amused and intrigued. I introduced them that day after class, and it was spontaneous combustion. Totally smitten with each other, they jabbered away, completely oblivious to me and the rest of the world.

For a while, I thought I had lost a friend. But I had really gained a new one. They are still happily married and still jabbering up a storm.

This success was a heady experience for me. Drunk with confidence, I launched matchmaking campaigns among my friends. The results were pleasant surprises. Many of my frisky introductions worked.

But some of them backfired. I had not yet learned that many young people, especially those in their early twenties, judge a book solely by its cover. For many of them, appearance and status are the only things that matter. I learned the dire effect of "glasses" or "pimples" or "working in the post office while going to college at night."

Some friends were positively insulted by the matches I attempted; but in looking back, I suspect it was more a reflection on them—because they never opened the book.

Among my early successes were two that made me think about matchmaking more seriously. When I got married, I acquired a whole new family—aunts, uncles, cousins, the entire spectrum. My wife had two cousins in their middle twenties, both very sweet girls, very shy, and dateless. My wife urged me to try to help. "There must be someone you know who'll appreciate them."

My world those days was full of bachelors—college and law school chums and many buddies—all looking for that certain someone. Actually finding husbands for the two cousins was pretty easy. One was married within a year; the other, about six months later. It was at the second wedding, while dancing with my wife, that I was summoned by her grandmother, the matriarch of the family, very old and much respected for her wisdom. She sat in a corner of the ballroom surrounded by an entourage of daughters, granddaughters, and great-granddaughters, as befitted her station. As I approached, she waved them all away and indicated that I was to sit alongside her. When we were alone, she said softly, "Milton, I want to thank you and bless you for helping my granddaughters and indeed through them the whole family. For this kind of work you will go straight to heaven when your time comes."

Not wanting to take any chances, I have kept matching to this day.

How a Matchmaker Works

I often surprise new friends and acquaintances when I tell them that I'm a dedicated matchmaker. This revelation usually elicits an incredulous "You must be kidding!" But it does get their attention. Once they realize that I am serious, they begin to listen with dreamy intentness.

More art than science, matchmaking is a blend of daring and intuition. When I meet someone new, the first question that runs through my mind is "Is she single?" or "Is he available?" The next question is "Who do I have for him or her?" I work on the premise that every unmarried woman is a sleeping princess, waiting for a prince's kiss, and every bachelor is looking for Miss Right. (Not Ms. Right! I've yet to meet a man who's looking for Ms. Right.) I run through all of the possible matchups until one of them clicks. If there's no click, I file them under "available" for future reference. I note and weigh all of the obvious considerations: age, education, appearance, religion, family, career, goals, and so forth.

Once a couple is paired in my mind, I try to find a way to bring them together. Most often a simple "Here's the number of a girl you ought to meet" is enough. But occasionally, I've needed more plotting than a soap opera script. I remember one particularly challenging case.

She was a disillusioned divorcée, and he was a jaded middle-aged businessman. They would no more think of going out on a blind date than of using someone else's toothbrush. I choreographed their meeting by arranging for them to be judges at a Beaux Arts ball. During the several hours they were thrown together, they "miraculously" discovered each other. I knew I had a winner when I got a New Year's card from him with a single word: "Thanks."

Frequently, the single people I'd like to help don't think they're lonely and don't want to get married. Occasionally, the couples I want to pair are already acquainted and don't even like each other! But I rarely let those details discourage me. I forge ahead, hopeful that fate is at work and that I'm just a tool of destiny.

My Turn

After practicing my calling for many years, it was my turn to receive the blessings of matchmaking. Fifteen years ago, my dear wife of more than twenty-five years died after a long illness. The devastation was incalculable. Everything was in disarray; nothing fit or made sense. I survived through the help and attention of my loving daughter Shelley and son-in-law Jim. They never let a week go by without involving me in their lives. I also had networks of wonderful people who propped me up every day—dear old friends, tennis buddies, daily commuter friends, my students at school, bridge partners, and, of course, my relatives.

Within weeks of my becoming a widower, there were people hard at work trying to find a match for me. Even my tailor got into the act. Although I turned down all suggestions for almost a year, I was not forgotten. Once I was ready to date, I was deluged with names and telephone numbers. (This is a more common occurrence for widowers than for widows, I'm told.) Unlike many singles who thumb their noses at blind dates, I was grateful for them. Each blind date presented a new adventure, a new exploration, a new opportunity: Maybe this will be it!

I was definitely looking for a wife. Many women couldn't believe it. It was ironic how often and how early on a date I was confidentially told, "I'm not interested in getting married. I'm really just interested in a relationship." This was probably done to put me at ease by assuring me that she was not a predatory female out to snare a vulnerable male in the clutches of matrimony.

I'd always respond by gently saying, "That's too bad. I'm looking for someone to marry. I couldn't bear to be stuck in just a relationship. I had such a happy marriage, and I certainly hope to be happily married again someday." (This statement invariably brought about a complete reversal in my date. "Oh," she'd cry. "Of course, I'd be happy to get married if I met the right man.")

But after months of dating, I began to get discouraged. I met some very lovely women but no one I could imagine sharing the rest of my life with. I had been a forlorn widower for well over a year when a good friend and fellow commuter came up to me one day on the station platform. She whispered in my ear, "I know a lovely woman. She's just right for you. Here's her phone number. Call her—you'll love her."

I did. And I do.

2

What Are You Really Looking For?

Part of the excitement of looking for someone to marry is that there are literally hundreds, maybe thousands, of possible partners for you: thousands of individuals you could build a happy, fulfilling life with as part of a married couple. They are not necessarily in your apartment house, neighborhood, or even in your town or state. But they are out there, and the smallest twist of fate or effort on your part can bring you face to face.

A woman friend of mine once told me in despair that she had just broken up with a man. "I'll never meet anybody like him again!" she wailed. No, of course she won't, because, thank heavens, nobody is exactly like anybody else. If you're looking for the Ideal Man or Woman, chances are you will not find that ideal. But do you want to search for an ideal or find a loving and lovable spouse?

When we narrow-mindedly decide that only one

kind of person is "appropriate" for us, we not only reduce our options, we also stultify and impoverish our lives. The adventure of looking for a mate encourages us to explore new ways of thinking about the world and ourselves. We must learn to discard some of the conventional thinking that is boxing us in.

My friend Deena is tyrannized by convention in this way. Deena looks and sounds very put together. Her job requires travel around the country. She enjoys her work and is good at it, but she has not been so successful at finding a person she could marry.

Deena's rigid thinking makes it hard for her to connect with someone. I once said to her, "I've got a wonderful man in mind for you. Here's his phone number. Give him a call." Deena looked at me with real alarm and said, "Oh, I could never do that. He has to call me first!"

One day at lunch, I presented a little puzzle to her. I drew something on a piece of paper, and when I handed it to her, her expression immediately betrayed her. She took no pleasure in the challenge. She said, "Oh, I hate tests!" I answered, "This isn't a test. It's a way to see things with a new pair of glasses."

This is what I handed Deena:

If you'd like to try to solve this puzzle, take a pencil

and without lifting it from the paper, draw four straight connected lines that go through all nine dots but through each dot only once. Try it now! Keep trying! If you can't reach a solution, turn to the end of this chapter.

Now that you know how it's done, you can see how easy it is. You could have solved it, but you added a condition that made it impossible to do so. No one told you not to go beyond the dots; that was a condition you imposed on yourself.

Some of the conditions and limitations in our lives are real, but many are self-imposed. We create hurdles by adopting "conventional behavior," which we think everyone observes. And indeed, adopting conventional behavior is the civilizing process. When we all observe the same rules and conventions, it makes it easier for society to survive. Nevertheless, we must be wise enough to examine what is best for us before we automatically follow the pack, just because that's what "they" say should be done. Don't be strangled by convention. The conventions we accept should spring out of our real interests and values, not from what others expect of us or from what we mistakenly believe we *ought* to do.

If I had a dollar for every man and woman who imposed conditions on himself or herself that made it harder to get married, I'd be very rich indeed!

There was one disastrous blind date that I arranged in college that still upsets me. To provide for my clothes and pocket money, I worked a shift on a street-corner newsstand. It was an extremely busy spot, and there were always three "newspaper boys" on hand to take care of the rush. Most of us were working our way through college, but there was one bright Italian guy who had been in the U.S. for only two years. Mike was great; he had mastered two languages, was attending night school, and gobbled up all of the books we recommended like jellybeans. He was a pleasure to talk to, funny and intelligent, with Continental charm. Dark, athletic, and extremely handsome, he was also very, very short. Even then I was sensitive to the fact that some women preferred tall men.

I shared a music appreciation class with a lovely girl named Teresa. She was intelligent, attractive, Italian, and not quite five feet tall. We sat alongside one another in class and occasionally shared a park bench when we ate our bag lunches. We liked one another as friends. I knew that she didn't date much, so when I suggested going out with my friend Mike on a double date, she was delighted. Mike and I were from the newsstand, and the two girls knew each other from college. I was high with excitement about the blind date. How would it work out? Within minutes of the introduction, I knew it was a bomb—Teresa froze. She stopped talking and interacting with us. She became a five-foot icicle. For a while Mike tried everything he could to make her laugh or join the conversation. Nothing worked, and soon he became silent too. The evening was a disaster.

As I suspected, Teresa was waiting for me in class on Monday. My weekend had not been wasted. I was prepared with a stunning defense that centered around the proposition that short men have a right to life too!

Imagine my surprise when she said, "You have some nerve setting me up with a date like that. No family, no education, no nothing. He's just an immigrant. I was born here! My mother was born here. Even my father came here as a very young child. It's insulting for you to think I'd have anything in common with him."

All of my protestations about his character, good looks, personality, and ambition fell on deaf ears. She was outraged.

Mike and I kept in touch. He went on to college at night, studied accounting, and finally became a partner in one of the Big Eight accounting firms. He's married with four grown children.

Teresa and I drifted apart, and I don't know what happened to her, but I still wonder whether she ever found an all-American husband.

Here's another example. Harry is short, by his own standards. If I tell Harry I've got a terrific woman for him—fun to be with, intelligent, and kind—this is his first question: "How tall is she?"

I hate to think about all of the wonderful tall women he'll never meet. Harry can't think outside the dots!

Here are two people making it harder for themselves to find someone with whom to spend the rest of their lives. Deena has decided that it's a crime for the woman to make the first move. What if, God forbid, her friends ever found out that she called the man first! It could nullify the whole marriage. Deena has decided to hang quietly on the wall, like a Mona Lisa with a faint smile, until Mr. Right comes along.

And how about Harry? Harry is five feet, seven inches. What if he fell in love with a wonderful woman who was five feet, ten inches? After they were married, what would happen? Would people run after them in the streets and say, "How awful! He's shorter than she is."

Ridiculous, isn't it? And yet we often shape our lives around such self-imposed, self-limiting hang-ups.

The Tyranny of Criteria

Establishing inflexible and unrealistic criteria for a marriage partner is one of the most destructive limitations we can choose. Alice, for example, is an intelligent and well-educated woman. She has come to the conclusion that she could be happy only with a man who is at least her intellectual equal. He must be brilliant and as mentally high-powered as she considers herself to be. Bert, on the other hand, has been poor all of his life, struggling very hard to achieve some financial success. When he marries, he wants to marry into a wealthy and important family. He will consider only a woman who can offer him this kind of upward mobility.

Perhaps Alice and Bert will be successful in their searches and wind up with exactly what they want. But by requiring these conditions as their key criteria, they limit the number of candidates they can consider. Alice and Bert are saying no to anyone who falls short of their narrow demands. They will miss the opportunities of a larger matrimonial pool.

We may not be aware of it, but we constantly screen our choices, assessing physical appearance, intelligence, personality, money, and social position. We may not even be aware of applying these tests; most often we make our judgments on a subliminal level. Instantly, we process a whole data bank of information—clothing, looks, speech, personality—and divide new people we meet into two groups: the "possible" and the "not possible." Fortunately, our initial assessments aren't permanent; they're subject to change as we pick up more data. However, if we don't allow our opinions to change, or if our criteria remain inflexible, then there are fewer and fewer potential partners.

What about you? Are your criteria so rigid they are severely narrowing your field of choice? How important is it to you that she be beautiful? That he be rich? That he or she be an athlete, a great cook, a good dancer, or a homebody? If you're a sculptor, will you consider dating a dentist? An entrepreneur? An accountant? If you're a corporate executive, will you consider a poet, a naturalist, a social worker? Maybe you've always been drawn to bookish intellectual types. Would you now consider going out with somebody who loves sports and prefers being out-of-doors?

Consider some of the common requirements people have for potential mates.

A preconceived notion about age is a primary one. And yet we're all living longer now and enjoying it more. There are men and woman in their eighties who seem young and others who are terminal fuddy-duddies at thirty. If you are past the childbearing stage of your life, age isn't all that important. Will there be adjustments to make between an older woman and a younger man? Of course. Will there be some compromises between an older man and a younger woman? Certainly. But compromise and adjustment are facts of life in anybody's marriage. If you find somebody on your wavelength, count your blessings, not the difference in years.

How About Physical Appearance?

Looks are everything to an adolescent, and some people never grow beyond this focus. They require good looks in a mate as an extension of their own egos. They show off their good-looking partners as if they were a new possession. "When I've got a beautiful woman on my arm," a man once said to me, "I feel like a million bucks." Well, maybe. But of course he won't be able to preserve this source of ego gratification forever after marriage. What happens when she has to rush to work in the morning, or feed the children, or weed the garden, or take the dog to the vet? She'll become an ordinary human being who sometimes gets tired and who looks less than perfect, at least occasionally. That won't do for a man who needs to feel like a million bucks. Not surprisingly, this man—and men and women like him—very rarely can find a suitable partner for a lifelong commitment.

We sometimes treat beauty or handsomeness as if it came from goodness or nobility within—a kind of award or badge of goodness. Alas, it's been my observation that very beautiful or handsome people often make terrible spouses!

Most of us are not "drop-dead lookers." We think of ourselves as "not bad-looking," yet we ironically keep searching for someone much better-looking than we are. A case in point: I once asked a lawyer friend, who had been divorced for several years, what kind of woman he was looking for. I was set back when he answered, passionately, "She's got to be gorgeous—a real stunner." I was surprised because he was such a homely specimen. By comparison, Woody Allen was tall, handsome, and at least had a full head of hair. Deciding to shake him up a bit, I said, "I know several women who might like to go out with you. One is a doctor, another is a concert musician, and a third is quite good-looking."

"How good-looking?" was his one question.

"Well," I said, "if you were in a restaurant with her, everyone would be looking at your table and thinking, What's a stunning-looking woman like that doing dating such a jerk?"

"That's the one I want," he replied.

So I gave him her phone number. When we met again several weeks later, I asked if he ever followed it up. "We set up a dinner date, and you were right. She is beautiful. Everyone in the restaurant was looking at us. But she's no heavyweight. I couldn't find anything to talk to her about. In fact she seemed really stupid. During the three hours we were together she kept fixing her face, checking her clothes, and scanning the room to see who was looking at her. A real disaster of a date! But I must confess, when I took her home, I decided I'd try for another date, but she said she was going to be busy for the balance of the century."

Some men and women never grow out of this adolescent preoccupation with good looks—even when it hinders them from developing truly satisfying relationships.

The old adage that "love is blind" means that love gives us a new pair of glasses. Love makes people more beautiful, not because we're blinded but because we see their deeper, truer selves. When we look at people with love, we see past their exterior, which may indeed be flawed or imperfect. You think that "inner beauty" is a cliché? Look at the face of a much-loved friend or family member whom you haven't seen for a while. Are you concerned with the size of the nose, the color of the eyes, the gray hair, or the wrinkles?

One of my favorite stories, illustrating the unimportance of appearance, is about Dolly, an old friend of my mother's. I first met her when I was four or five years old. I was terrified yet fascinated by her appearance. As a child, she had fallen into a fire, and some of her face had been burned away. Her nose and upper lip were just scar tissue. A face to frighten anyone. Nevertheless, I was quickly drawn to her. She was gentle and kind, with a quick understanding and a warming laugh. In time I completely forgot about her mutilated face, and as I grew older, I resented anyone who stared at her. She often brought her two younger boys to play with me while she had tea with my mother.

How did she ever get married? Her husband, Ben, was a highly successful business broker. He should have had no problem finding a wife except that he was fat, very fat. Most of the women who wanted to marry him were attracted only by his money. But he was well aware of this, and, of course, he wanted something more.

Then he had a heart attack. In intensive care, he was ministered to by round-the-clock nurses, including a young nurse who always wore a surgical mask when she entered the room. Her name was Dolly, and she was the sweetest, kindest, most understanding woman he had ever met. During her shift, they spent hours talking together. Then one day he asked her to remove her mask. "All the other nurses have taken their masks off," he said. "Why haven't you?"

Dolly began to weep quietly. Ben put his arm around her to learn what the problem was. Weeping, Dolly told him, then took off her mask. "Dolly," Ben said, "I don't care about your face, I care about you. And let's face it, I'm no Adonis myself. You like the me inside and I love the you behind your face. Will you marry me?" She said yes, and they were happily married ever after and brought up three wonderful children. Now that's a true fairy tale.

Intelligence

Intelligence is a wonderful faculty. It makes for curiosity about the world; it can produce understanding and insight. But there are many different types of intelligence. There are book smarts and street smarts, business shrewdness and psychological insight. Some intelligent people lack empathy and understanding. One man told me that intelligence in a woman had always been a crucial criterion for him. When I asked him what he meant by intelligence, he said that his last girlfriend had a law degree. However, he added, somehow she never understood him. I wonder if he has ever figured out that intelligence and understanding don't always go hand in hand.

For twelve years, my friend Terry was married to the man of her dreams—on paper. "I wanted a man who was very, very respected intellectually, and Bob had all the right credentials: private schools, a Ph.D. from

Princeton, a big-time job in Washington, a great resumé! But inside, he was a deeply insecure man. I spent twelve years trying to cheer him up. We were miserable together and finally divorced. The man I'm with now is Bob's complete opposite. Jack didn't finish college. He owns his own business. He loves trout fishing and driving jeeps and watching baseball. That doesn't sound like me at all, does it? But the fact is he's really smarter than Bob is in most ways I care about. Not in book learning. But he loves life and is profoundly interested and curious about the world. He's open-minded and he's not at all threatened by my intellectual pursuits."

Paul was a delightful fellow who thrilled all of his friends and family as he grew into an international scholar. He didn't marry, although he could well afford marriage and was eager to start a family. His key criteria for a wife were academic credentials and an I.Q. in the stratosphere. Paul used that standard for every woman he met, and the years rolled by. Not surprisingly, he had never managed to find a woman who lived up to his lofty requirements. Nobody could pass through the eye of his needle.

Paul was thirty-eight when we had a talk. I had already arranged several dates for him but they didn't end in romance. Although the women met his rigid academic criteria, so much more was missing.

"Paul, what do you want from a wife?" I asked.

Despite his eminence, Paul is very shy, and he answered with embarrassment, "I would expect her to be my best friend, to love me, and permit me to love her."

"Fine," I said. "But how in the world does the fact

that a woman is a professor or a famous author qualify her for what you just described in a wife? Do intellectuals make better lovers? Believe me, if you find somebody who can become your best friend, it won't matter whether she's a receptionist or a brain surgeon."

Paul agreed, and I arranged a blind date with a warm and charming woman who works in a department store. They like each other very much. Time will tell.

How About Money and Status?

Sure, money is important. Who can disagree with my late father-in-law, who offered this advice to me when I was a very young man: "Milton, it's better to be rich and healthy than poor and sick." But the fact is money can't make you either healthy or happy. The C.D.s in the bank, the title on the door, the monogram on the handkerchief—none of these will warm you in the cold winter nights of life.

I recall an encounter with a status-conscious woman. I was very mean to her, but I confess that the recollection brings nothing but satisfaction and a sly smile. I was boarding a commuter train after work one day and found myself, in the hurly-burly of getting a seat, next to a pretty young lady. For the first fifteen minutes or so, we were both busy with our newspapers. Then she drew out a set of typed papers from her briefcase and began to work.

"Aha," I said. "So you're an editor?"

She responded with a friendly laugh: "No, I teach

English literature in college, and this is a term paper I'm grading."

In the next half hour, we learned a great deal about each other. When she discovered that I was happily married, a father, and an amateur matchmaker, she confided her story to me. She was in her early thirties, successful, single, and anxious to marry. Somehow she had never met the right man.

"I find that hard to believe," I said. "You're attractive, intelligent, successful, and you obviously can talk comfortably with people. Maybe you want too much. If you take this train every day, there are dozens of men you might meet."

"Well," she said, "I did meet one very interesting man several months ago. He was a redhead with an infectious laugh. He was a wonderful conversationalist; there wasn't a subject I could bring up that he didn't know something about or wasn't interested in. He was also the most well-read man I've ever met."

"Sounds great," I offered.

"That's not all. He was single and appeared to be looking for marriage and a family. It all seemed too good to be true—and it was."

"What was wrong?"

"When I asked him what he did for a living, he said he ran a gas station."

"What's wrong with that?" I wanted to know.

"How could I fall in love with a man who runs a gas station? How could I introduce him to my friends or family? How would I ever explain it?"

"And yet, he seemed perfect in every other way?"

"A gas station attendant—you must be kidding. I'm glad I didn't give him any encouragement. In fact, I turned him down when he asked for my phone number."

We rode along in silence for several minutes. I was depressed by our conversation. I guess I couldn't help but empathize with the fellow. Then I saw my station coming up, and the train started to slow down. I decided to be naughty. I turned to her and asked, "Did he have freckles?"

"Yes, he did. Why?"

"Good Lord, I know him. I've played tennis with him. We call him Red. When he said he ran a gas station, he was being very modest because he owns thirty-seven of them. He's one of the largest independent dealers in the state." The train pulled up to the station, and as I made my way down the aisle, I turned and waved to my stricken friend. One hand was over her mouth and her look seemed to say, "What have I done?"

I'm sure she would never believe that status and money control her romantic life, but of course they do.

Going beyond rigid criteria of status, beauty, intelligence, and age can help you find love and happiness. It makes the adventure of searching for a mate more exciting and open-ended. Can you shake up your thinking a little bit?

See what happens when you think outside the dots.

Marriage and the Empty Train: A Parable

Once upon a time, there was a woman (or perhaps it was a man) who stood on a railroad platform

*waiting for a train. She was filled with anticipa-
tion as the train came roaring into the station.
She was off to the city! The train stopped, and the
doors opened. What kind of seat would she get?
That would make all of the difference in her
enjoyment of the trip. The woman rushed into the
car and was thrilled to see that all of the seats
were empty. She could sit anyplace she wanted.
But then the problem surfaced. Which was the best
seat for her?*

*The window seats had better light and a view
of the countryside. But the outdoor light was often
broken up by passing buildings and trees, which
made reading difficult. Then, as the train approached the city, the scenes became dull or depressing. The aisle seats had uniform light and
an armrest. And it was easier to get in and out
of them. But she'd be disturbed when the person
in the window seat got in or out. Then there was
the problem of which row. She knew, of course,
that the center of the car had the least vibration
and sway, but it had the worst light----no windows.
Center seats were farthest from the exits, and so it
would take her longer to get out.*

*She was walking up and down the aisle
trying to make the best choice when the train
reached the next station. Many new passengers
got on and quickly took their seats. She was
dismayed to see that some of the "best seats" were
taken. Her choices were becoming considerably
smaller. Undaunted, she continued to ponder
which of the remaining seats she wanted. Alas,
each seat was unique, each seat had its pros and*

cons, and before she finally made up her mind, the train stopped again and picked up more passengers. Soon there were only a few seats left. In a bit of a panic, she settled on one of the remaining seats, mindful that she never would have chosen it when the train first came in but relieved that she had gotten one of the few seats left. Once she had settled down, she realized that her choice was not so bad: she was comfortably seated at last, relaxed, and on her way to her destination. She couldn't help noticing that there were a few passengers who preferred to stand rather than sit in a seat that wasn't quite perfect. "How dumb," she thought.

*   *   *

Here is the answer to the nine-dot puzzle earlier in the chapter.

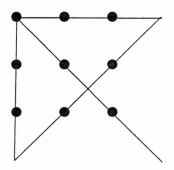

3

Where Are They?

L ooking for someone to marry isn't a competition or a marathon. It can be an adventure—possibly the greatest adventure of your life. To engage in it, you don't have to race up Heartbreak Hill or break any records. The process is fun. It's exciting. Approach it with zest and curiosity, and you will have the time of your life.

The opportunities for meeting that certain someone are limited only by the boundaries of your imagination. But one thing is certain—this process is like the lottery: You have to be in it to win it. What is the good of sitting alone in your room? Join the parade.

Go Where the Fish Are

If you want to succeed at fishing, you go where the fish are. No matter how great your bait or lure, you're not going to catch any fish in your bathtub. So give yourself a break. Cast your net in waters that have the greatest potential. For example, there are certain activities that draw men. You'll find men at sporting events, playing tennis, golf, or handball, jogging around the track, and working out at the gym. Also fishing. Fly- and deep-sea-fishing fans are almost exclusively men. You'll find women at concerts, dance recitals, lectures, and museums. The odds are against finding a potential wife at a hockey match or fight arena. And if you're looking for a husband, you'd do better somewhere other than a rally sponsored by NOW or the annual Weaver's Christmas exhibit. And yet I'm sure there is a small chance for romance even in those unlikely meeting places.

There is probably no activity or arena that is completely out of bounds. The spark can be triggered anywhere, anytime you have a man and a woman.

The important thing is to keep what I call your "antenna d'amour" tuned in. Have you ever noted that when the car radio is switched on, nothing happens for several moments; then, as the retractable antenna starts to extend, you get static until the antenna is all the way up; and finally you begin to get a clear signal of music or speech. Too many of us keep our love antenna switched off. We make it almost impossible to pick up those vital signals of interest and availability that are needed for romance to flower.

Sharing a common goal opens up opportunities for more personal sharing. Sharing a learning experience can be fun: learn to play bridge or tennis, to skate or ski, or improve your dancing or become fluent in Spanish.

Are you passionate about the environment, the homeless, nuclear war, the Democrats, the Republicans, the Chicago Cubs, or even the Dewey Decimal System? Working with others to achieve any goal opens new doors and uncovers new opportunities.

I especially recommend continuing education classes at your local college or community center. The art courses attract many women; science attracts mostly men. To find a balance of both men and women, pick a class in writing or natural history, money management or changing careers, computers or "auto repair for poets." If nothing else, at least you'll learn something!

Taking a course helps you cut corners. It's very easy to talk to fellow students. You start out with something in common. And people who take classes are generally winners; they're trying to improve themselves or their job opportunities. They're curious; they have a zest for life.

Some years ago my class in Applied Creativity was completely filled. Just before the first class was about to begin, a young woman dashed into the classroom and breathlessly asked to speak to me. She was quite agitated, so I stepped into the hall and closed the door behind me.

"I *must* take your course, Mr. Fisher."

"The class is completely filled. Perhaps you can take it next term."

"Let me explain. I'm in the middle of getting a divorce, and I'm under great stress. My therapist suggested I take the course to help me get through this terrible period in my life."

"But there are literally no more seats," I told her.

"That's OK. I'll bring a pillow and sit on the floor."

That seemed like such an enterprising solution that I relented. The young woman joined the class and proved to be an excellent student and an asset to the class.

Her divorce became final before the end of the semester, and she eventually married one of the men she met in the class.

Look in Your Own Backyard

When I was a child, I read a story about a man who spent his whole life looking for a four-leaf clover. When he was just starting out in life, an elf told him a four-leaf clover would bring him good luck. He searched the entire world for this clover, giving up everything—career, marriage, and family—in his fevered quest. But his search was to no avail. At last, old, tired, and broken, he returned to his old house to find everyone gone. With tears in his eyes, he sat on the doorstep and stared at the ground. And there at his feet was the four-leaf clover he had been searching for all of his life.

Do some of us waste a lifetime looking for a treasure that is right at our doorstep? There may be someone nearby who could be that special person in your life, but you're looking elsewhere. A flower doesn't have to be exotic to be beautiful. Take another look.

Here's a story that expresses this point. David was a widower. After his wife's death, David didn't go out on a date for well over a year. When he did start to date, the women were all very pretty and much younger than he was. Some were ten years younger, some even twenty. He took satisfaction in seeing the envious expressions on the faces of his colleagues and friends when they met his dates.

Nevertheless, the young women were all out of sync with David. What he thought important they trivialized. The things that impressed them left him bored. So after a while he stopped dating. He had a small circle of friends, played poker once a week, and kept up with his relatives.

He did have one good friend, a woman named Diana who lived in the same building. Diana had been very helpful during his wife's illness. She still lived in the same apartment she had shared with her ex-husband before he ran off with his secretary. Diana and David took the same bus each morning and had shared each other's problems throughout the years. They trusted and respected one another.

One morning Diana got to the bus stop and David wasn't there. Since he was usually early, Diana decided to run back to his apartment and see what was wrong. After many rings on the doorbell, a very bedraggled and sniffly David answered the door.

"I was up all night, and I can't go to work today," David explained.

"Is there anything I can do for you?"

"I'll be OK," David said rather miserably. "I've got some cough syrup and stuff."

Diana went off to work, and David went back to bed. That evening he was lying in bed when he heard a knock at the door. There was Diana with a napkin-covered tray of delicious food.

"I brought you something to get your strength back," Diana said. "There's some chicken soup. I confess it's Campbell's. I didn't have time to make it from scratch. And some chicken breasts with rice and mushroom gravy." David hadn't eaten all day and suddenly he was aware of being hungry.

"I'll make some hot tea to go with the angel cake," Diana said. In a few moments, she had set the table, and David was beginning to feel better as he spooned up the chicken soup.

Then suddenly, for no apparent reason, a tear ran down his face, then another and another. Diana was startled.

"My goodness, David, what's the matter?"

David put down his spoon, looked deep into her eyes, and said simply, "Diana, I'm such a jerk!"

After they married, they gave up both apartments and started out fresh in Florida. They are one of the happiest couples I know.

You may even find that somebody you snubbed yesterday may be perfect for you a few years down the road! I know one couple who first met in their teens when she was a senior camper and he was a junior counselor. It was hate at first sight. She thought he was a stuck-up snob and he thought she was a scrawny spoiled brat.

I didn't know any of this when it occurred to me that these two were meant for each other. I suggested that he call her for a date, and so it was that he showed up at her door. Five years had passed, and neither of them remembered the other's name. But as soon as she saw him, she recognized him and fled to her bedroom. Her mother followed her to find out what the trouble was.

"I know him and I hate him," the young woman exclaimed.

Her sensible mother said, "You can't break your date at the last minute. Anyway, he seems like a nice young man, and he comes well recommended."

Her mother was right. Of course, both of them had changed with the years. They fell in love and were married within a year. Twenty-five years later, we helped them celebrate their silver wedding anniversary.

Another example is Pete, my old college chum. In college, Pete was insulted when Eileen showed an interest in him. He considered her completely inappropriate—she was too fat for one thing.

"But, Pete, she's very nice, a lot of fun," I told him.

"Forget it," he said. After all, he was on the football team and in the Drama Club, very popular and much pursued. Who was she? Nobody. Some nerve!

After graduation, Peter married one of the stars of the Drama Club. They both landed parts in Broadway shows and for a time were the most famous couple from our class. As the years went by, Pete's wife became a real star, and he faded into an occasional appearance on a TV commercial. The marriage didn't last, and Pete began to drift professionally. To keep going, he did what so many actors do; he got a job as a waiter. He worked the lunch shift in an exclusive private club. One day, he was stunned to see Eileen as the guest of one of the club's most prominent members. She was as cheerful and nice as ever and just as plump.

Anxiously, he approached her table, wondering whether she would recognize and acknowledge him or snub him. She seemed delighted to see him and said,

"Hello, Pete, you look wonderful." He broke into a bashful smile and said, "Eileen, you're a sight for sore eyes."

Pete took their order, and as he left their table, he overheard her say, "He was the leading man in my life all through college."

When he finished work, the maître d' handed him a note. It read: "I'd love to talk about the old days. Give me a call. Eileen." And on the note was her phone number in Manhattan.

Eileen was still smitten, and now, after years had passed, Pete had matured and was ready. They began to date, got married, had two children, and went into the travel agency business together. They appear to be very successful and happy.

Should You Advertise?

Consider the great American tradition, advertising. Talk about adventure! Put an ad in one of the personals columns and see what it brings. Let them know who you are and what you seek.

Some people shrink from the mere thought of advertising themselves. How demeaning! How crass! What if somebody should find out they were advertising to find a mate?

Ridiculous! In fact, a personal ad is simply a way to negotiate your own blind dates. It's a way to move ahead without waiting for some friend or relative to think of you. There are many advantages to the personal ad:

1. It's impersonal. The ad never gives your name
   and address. The response is to a P.O. box or
   an impersonal mail drop. The respondent
   takes the step of revealing himself or herself
   first. You may screen the respondents safely.
   Of course, you may decide to be the re-
   sponder. This may take a little more guts, but
   it's also free and fast. Buy the newspaper or
   magazine tonight, peruse the columns, and tomorrow you can have a letter winging its way toward adventure.
2. It is targeted to reach a preselected market.
   The very fact that someone is reading the personals indicates he or she is interested in establishing a relationship. And generally, those who
   are not interested in marriage say so.
3. It lets you further target your market by putting up front the criteria you think are absolutely essential. The wonderful thing about
   advertising of any kind is that you can tailor
   your ad to reach a specific group and eliminate
   others. In marketing, this is called establishing
   a niche. You can define the niche any way you
   want to: college grad, opera lover, good cook,
   nonsmoker, even mother of two!
4. It gives you a chance to put potential dates on
   notice about things you are anxious about—
   your height, weight, or age—or feel strongly
   about—career, religious beliefs, or political
   commitments. If you are overweight, for example, why not get the hurdle of your size out of
   the way in your ad? Then you don't have to

worry about its effect on your date when you
meet for the first time.

Advertising isn't a one-shot deal. Successful adver-
tisers know they get the best results from many ads. So
don't be discouraged if you don't hit the jackpot right
away. Study the ads of others. Change your ad and see
what happens. Did you get more or fewer responses?
Why did this ad draw so many wrong people?

My observation is that many people don't give
enough time and thought to their ads. They just adapt
someone else's ad because they think it sounds good,
overlooking the reality of who they are, what they're
looking for, and what they can realistically hope for.
Placing this kind of ad is an exercise in daydreaming,
pleasant while you're doing it but not destined to
achieve any goals.

Most people tend to glamorize themselves in ads,
and a little judicious hype is probably not a bad thing.
Others, however, have a hard time being fair to themselves. I persuaded one woman, a widow in her early
fifties, to place an ad, and she subsequently chided me
when she got only one response. When I asked to see
her ad, I was appalled to read this: "Widow, middle-
aged, honest, good housekeeper, looking for a man with
a steady job or good pension; must be very neat."

Surely an ad to stir the romantic wellsprings in any
man! I persuaded the widow to rewrite her ad, and
together we came up with this: "Widow, no children,
happily married for twenty years, financially independent, seeks nonsmoker who loves dancing and still
has goals to reach."

The first appearance of the new ad brought eight

responses, which resulted in five dates, one of which created a relationship that went on for seven months. So far, she's not married, but she's having a good time. She's doing something—and she's getting results.

The Singles Weekend

Resort areas often organize singles weekends, and this is a wonderful way to meet people. Like advertising in a personals column, going on such a weekend lets you meet people who are also interested in meeting people! In addition, you get to enjoy swimming, sports, country walks, good food, and dancing.

If you can think of these weekends as networking opportunities as well as mate-finding ones, you can have fun and a successful time even if you don't meet the woman or man of your dreams.

My cousin Stan told me about his strategy—actually his nonstrategy—at singles weekends: "I go to have a good time, pure and simple. If I meet somebody, great. If I don't, that's OK too. Since I feel that way, I generally *do* meet some interesting women. I'm dating a wonderful woman right now that I met last spring at a singles weekend. It was funny: I hate to dance; she loves it. I love to eat; she's always on a diet. But we found out we love to talk to each other!" Take the pressure off yourself. You're there to have fun.

Be a Matchmaker Yourself

Maybe it's naive, but I believe that helping other people makes you lucky. Helping other people on any level brings rich rewards in addition to the pleasure of doing good. People remember you; they think about you, and they try to help you.

Being a matchmaker yourself is one of the best ways you can build an army of supporters. Have you ever tried to bring two people together? If you haven't, try it! There's tremendous satisfaction when you introduce two people—and the spark is there! It's dramatic proof that what you do can make a difference. And it's a terrific way to get the ball rolling for yourself. The number of people you can meet is enormously increased when you have a network of people who like you and want to help. It's exciting and heartwarming to know that there are friends and relatives who are keeping you in mind.

Anywhere, Anytime

If you're open to the possibilities, you can meet someone anywhere, anytime! I had a student once who was a lonely, discouraged widow. She took my course to "get back in the stream of life." I chatted with her one day after class and asked her, "Were you happily married?" "Oh, yes," she replied. "We had our differences, but he was my best friend."

"You should find someone and get married again."

"You're a great kidder, Milton," she said. "Look at me. I know I'm not a great beauty, I've got varicose veins and old-fashioned ideas, and a millionaire I'm not. What would anyone see in me?"

"Think positive," I told her. "You never can tell."

About six months later, my lonely widow ran up to me at the train station with a nice-looking middle-aged gentleman in tow. Before I could even say hello, she blurted out, "Meet my fiancé." She showed me an impressive ring on her left hand. "We're getting married in November and going to Florida for our honeymoon."

As her gentleman chatted with the others in our party, I was able to whisper, "Where did you meet him?"

"In the lamp section of Bloomingdale's," she answered. "He was standing there looking so confused and lost that I just walked over and asked him if he needed any help. He told me he was a recent widower and that he needed a lamp for his new apartment. I helped him pick out a nice contemporary floor lamp, and told him Macy's was having a sale on rugs. Pretty soon we were chatting away, and he asked me out." She lowered her voice and added, rather shyly, "He's a lovely man and he thinks I'm beautiful, varicose veins and all."

Where do you meet people? Anytime and anywhere.

Clifford was a bachelor in his mid-thirties who lived in a medium-size Connecticut town. He wanted to get married, but he never seemed to find the time—or the right girl. He had just been promoted to an executive level, and his first big assignment took him to Caracas, Venezuela. After a week of business negotiations in Spanish, Clifford found himself free to sightsee. He decided to seek out what had been described as "the eighth wonder of the world"—a cable car ride that went to the top of one of the world's highest mountains.

Clifford took his place in line on the platform, waiting for the next cable car, when he was thrilled to hear the women in front of him speaking English. How he had missed it! Once the passengers were seated and the doors locked, the usually shy Clifford spoke to one of the women. "Are you from the U.S.?" he asked.

"Yes," she replied, "Connecticut."

"What a coincidence. That's where I live," Clifford said. "What town?"

"Hamden. How about you?"

"That really is a coincidence. I'm from Hamden, too!"

Then the woman exclaimed, "You must be Clifford Bowen!"

Clifford was staggered. He had very few friends, was fairly new to Hamden, and didn't think anyone knew or cared.

The woman's name was Caroline, and she explained it all. Just before she left for her long-planned spring vacation in Caracas, she had read an item in the local paper describing Clifford's forthcoming trip to Venezuela. She even had said to herself, "Wouldn't it be funny if I met him?"

They spent as much time as they could together for the remainder of their stay. The magic of their meeting changed their lives, and they've now been happily married for several years.

Another magic incident changed the life of my friend Agatha. She was a teacher in her mid-thirties who often volunteered to be a faculty chaperone at the student dances. She loved the dancing, the music, and the happy, excited faces of the dressed-up seniors.

At one of these dances, there was a door prize offered—two tickets to *Hello, Dolly!* on Broadway. When the drawing was held, Agatha jumped up when she heard them read out the winning number—14587! It was hers! She dashed up to the platform.

But when she handed her ticket to the student M.C., he handed it back to her with great embarrassment: "Miss Johnson, your number is 14578. The winning number is 14587. I'm sorry."

Agatha left the platform as the M.C. continued to call out the winning number. After a minute or so, a tall bespectacled gentleman with graying temples went up to the platform. He was Roger Scott, one of the parents who had come to chaperone.

Overcome with embarrassment, Agatha made her way to the cloakroom. As she was struggling into her coat, she became aware that someone was assisting her. It was Mr. Scott.

Gently and shyly, he said, "I'm so sorry you didn't win. Everything about you spells winner. I hope you won't think me presumptuous, but I'd like to share that prize with you. I'm divorced, and I'd love to take you to see *Hello, Dolly!*"

They went to the show together and enjoyed it thoroughly, as well as each other's company. They have been married now for fourteen years.

I know of no activity or arena that is completely out of bounds. The spark can be triggered anywhere, anytime. Sometimes it's by sheer accident, pure chance, dumb luck. But even then you must recognize the opportunity knocking at your door. Be sensitive to the world around you and the messages it has for you. You cannot, however, let your whole life and future depend on luck. You had best do something about it.

Wherever your journey through life takes you, you will meet people. The richer your life experience, the wider your interests, the deeper your commitment, the greater the potential for meeting and matching. Ironically, if your sole interest and activity is looking for a spouse, you will probably be doomed to frustration. When all you do is focus on "marriage hunting," you label yourself as narrow, self-centered, and uninteresting. Not the best packaging to present to the world. It's an image that will frighten away the very ones you're seeking.

To paraphrase an old Scottish saying, "Don't go after a spouse—but go where the potential spouses are."

4

The Catalyst Connection

D o you believe that it has to be love at first
sight—or it's not the real thing? Alas, many
people do. They believe that the chemistry of
love is spontaneous combustion, something like a sky-
rocket, fireworks, or sparklers.

They are sadly mistaken. Of all of the people I've
queried, fewer than 1 percent claimed their marriage
started with love at first sight. However, it's such a
romantic myth that even that 1 percent may be rewriting
history.

Hundreds of interviews with happily married people have led me to the conclusion that, when examined
in retrospect, some small isolated factor changed the
two people involved, drew them together, and ultimately helped in their discovery that they were in love.

I call this factor the catalyst. The dictionary defines
catalyst as a substance, usually present in small amounts,
that modifies or increases the rate of a chemical reaction. In effect, the catalyst begins the mysterious process
of romance! The catalyst makes you realize that here is
something special—for you.

The catalyst can be any one of a thousand things, from a shared love of poetry to a talent for tap dancing, from an avid interest in computer programming to the ability to fix a child's toy or bake a great pie. It may involve only one of the individuals, but that may be enough to create a positive change in the other.

My mother believed the catalyst for her was my father's energy and charismatic effect on people. She once told me, "He gave life to any gathering. And he gave so much life to my life."

The Little Things in Life Count, Too

For Harry, the catalyst was chess. Harry knew a dozen women, each of whom could qualify as a wife. They were all attractive enough, intelligent enough, friendly enough, and they met all of Harry's criteria in reasonable measure. He liked them all, he dated them all, and he was equally interested in each of them in a casual sort of way. Then one day, Harry discovered that Sally played chess. She learned as a child and used to play with her late father. Harry played a game with her, and although he beat her, he was impressed with her intelligence and depth. Her ability and passion for the game and the challenge it presents intrigued Harry, and he saw Sally in a new light. He began to realize that she was really more simpatico, affectionate, and fun to be with than any of the other women in his life. Lo and behold, the catalyst had done its work.

The catalyst factor for Sally may have been that Harry, all of a sudden, is obviously in love with her. He now makes her feel important and desirable. Sally's reaction is "How can you help loving a guy like that?" So they're off on the road to building a life together!

I've asked hundreds of happily married people, "What was the catalyst in your romance?" The answers have been as interesting and varied as the shells on the beach.

I recently asked two men about their marriages. One, a tennis pro, is young and handsome and obviously was at no loss for girlfriends in his single days. He told me, "The one thing that drew me to my wife was the fact that she is so neat and well organized. I'm emotional and impulsive, a bit of a slob, and she's kind of like a rock, very rational and controlled. I realized we'd make a great couple. We've been married for seven years and are very happy."

My other friend is a middle-aged widower who recently remarried. I asked him, "What was the catalyst for you? You'd been a widower for five years and dated a bushel of women. What made your new wife different?"

Henry said, "I never really thought about it and I don't know." The next day he called and said, "You know, her laugh reminded me of my mother's, and I think that started it."

Maria works as a cashier at a luncheonette. She's in her late thirties, happily married, and has a son now entering college. About the catalyst for her marriage, she says: "It's a long story. I was seventeen and went to a dance with my big sister. It was crowded, with the girls on one side of the room and the boys on the other side. The music started to play, and some of the fellows came across the floor to ask for a dance. Nobody in our crowd had been asked yet when an older guy on the other side of the room started talking to his friend. I couldn't hear him, but I was sure he was talking about me. He kept looking and looking, and I pretended I was fixing my shoe. Sure enough he came over and asked me to dance. He was a very good dancer and nicely dressed and twenty-four years old! Later that night he took my name and number, and we started to date. It was exciting and fun, but then after four or five months I got scared. He was so serious, and I still wanted to go out with different men, so I broke it off.

"Then, for about a year, I dated a lot. Some of the guys liked me, but I didn't like them. Most of them were out to get whatever they could. Anyway, one Saturday afternoon I was in the kitchen ironing, and I had just said to my mother, 'You remember that first older guy who took me out last year? He was real nice,' when — it's really true! — the phone rang, and it was he. He told me he was getting his good suit out to go to the cleaners when he found the slip of paper on which I had written my name and number.

"We started to date again and really fell in love. We've been married nineteen years now, have two kids, one just starting college, and we own this place. See the chef over there? That's my husband and partner!

"What made the difference? Well, he respected me. Treated me like I was somebody. He wasn't interested in just a fast romance. He was serious, he was thinking of me as his wife, and I began to think about him as a husband."

When somebody wants to marry you, that's a powerful catalyst.

Shared Passions

People who are passionate about anything, whether a hobby, a sport, a political cause, music, art, food, people, dance, or religion, have a better chance at the catalyst connection. The boundless enthusiasm, the ardent interest, the fervor and zeal of an aficionado who really cares about something, is like the fragrance of a flower: it attracts and motivates.

Enthusiasts are interesting and different, with special knowledge and special goals. Sharing their interests can broaden your life. You may become an aficionado yourself.

One friend's story is a fine example of this point. Many years ago her grandparents met, fell in love, and married under the following circumstances. Fred was a Harvard University graduate, very intellectual and literary, with an inquisitive mind. He was fascinated by the world and how it works but was more of a spectator than a participant. Bess, on the other hand, was an immigrant who had come through Ellis Island as an eight-year-old child and had survived and even thrived in the teeming life of the Lower East Side of New York. She had managed to get through public school and high school and complete two years of college before the financial straits of her family forced her into full-time work. She had always worked part-time, but now this was not enough. With it all, Bess was thoroughly Americanized, with a heart that resonated to all of the misery and injustice she saw around her. She was an activist. She joined parades, signed petitions, and helped wherever she could.

One day there was a great rally. "Free Tom Mooney" was its theme. Tom Mooney, a prominent labor leader, was in prison on apparently trumped-up charges. Liberals throughout the country raised a hue and cry to free him. The auditorium was packed, all anxious to hear the fiery speakers and enjoy the program of entertainers who had volunteered to help.

Fred took an aisle seat in the balcony so that he could observe the audience as well as the program. Bess was an usherette with handbills and leaflets to distribute. She also had a can to collect donations to "Free Tom Mooney."

When she reached Fred's seat, she gave him a leaflet and presented the can for a donation. He sniffed and just turned away, outraged at this brash invasion of his privacy. What a mistake! Bess was on him like a tiger with a staccato stream of words that described the injustice done to Tom Mooney and the need for real Americans, for real human beings, to help, to stand up to tyranny and insist on justice. Fred withdrew in his seat as far as he could, but there was no place to hide. All he could manage was a rather feeble "I don't know the man and I don't know the facts. I've only come to observe. All of this has nothing to do with me."

"That's what you think, you ostrich! Go ahead and hide; maybe it will go away!" And with that Bess turned her back on him and stalked away.

Fred stayed for the whole program, but he didn't hear a thing. He was stunned and shaken by her emotional outburst. How could she care so much? Was there something wrong with him? Was he too remote, too rational?

For several weeks after the rally, he continued to

think of the encounter and all that he might have said to justify his position. Then one day, while browsing at the library on Fifth Avenue, he spotted Bess at a library table, surrounded by a pile of books and working on a paper. With considerable trepidation he approached the table. When she looked up, he timidly said, "I don't know whether you remember me, but we met at the 'Free Tom Mooney' rally."

"Of course I do," she responded rather sadly. "You're the ostrich, the guy who thinks misery has nothing to do with him."

Fred was destroyed. His worst fears about whether to approach her had come true. He backed away and edged out of the library. In a kind of daze he took the subway home. After two stations, he suddenly pulled himself together and mused: She's such an interesting woman, fiery, smart, and compassionate. Maybe I am an ostrich! He dashed out of the subway and hurried back to the library. Would she still be there? Fortunately, she was. Fred summoned all of his courage and approached the table again. She looked up, and he said, "I've come back to help Tom Mooney. Will you go out with me?" She did and they ended up happily married for fifty-seven years. Bess continues to fight for justice.

Tragedy and Timing

For Walter, the catalyst was a tragedy in his youth. Walter is a slight, shy man with dark, attractive eyes and a self-effacing smile. Married for twenty-five years, he told me, "I'm sure I could have married one of many other women and achieved a happy marriage, but Ida is special, especially now, because we've gone through so much together.

"The catalyst? Well, I guess it was when my father died during my last term in college. My mother had passed away when I was thirteen, and my father had raised me and my younger sister. I had known Ida and her family for years. In fact, she was tutoring me in math to make sure I could get all my credits and graduate. After my father's death, there was sheer chaos in our lives. Ida stepped in and helped. She always seemed to know what to do. She encouraged me to keep our house and to graduate. She was, in fact, a lot like my father — gregarious, friendly, and full of quiet confidence. I began to see her in a different light. We got married when I was twenty-one. It was the best move I ever made."

In an interview with Ida, she told me, "The catalyst for me was that he needed me. And he was so dependable and honest and grateful. He took his responsibilities very seriously, and I admired and loved him for it."

Lola's story could easily have had an unhappy ending. Lola is a successful, charming, and still beautiful woman. She has carved out a unique career for herself. She is a cosmetics demonstrator who is so effective a famous company flies her around the country to teach other demonstrators how to sell their cosmetics.

When asked what was the catalyst that led to her marriage, she recalled, "I was a very free spirit when I was younger. After I graduated from college, I wanted to go to medical school and become a psychiatrist. My parents just laughed, and my father said, 'One doctor in the family is enough. At least your brother is serious. He didn't drop out of college every time he wanted some adventure. Get a job, get married, settle down.'

"So I picked myself up and went to Italy, and for the next few years I lived by my wits. I must have had twenty jobs and at least as many boyfriends. I developed a special technique whenever one of the wealthy middle-aged bachelors made a pass at me: I'd move in with him. He'd be so shocked he wouldn't know what to do. My life consisted of parties, gifts, excitement, and sheer terror between boyfriends.

"Finally, I had enough. My parents were distraught, and I missed them and the United States. When I came home, my family treated me lovingly albeit a bit gingerly.

"One day, my grandmother, whom I loved very much, asked me to have lunch with her and an Italian-speaking friend. I showed up and discovered that Grandma's friend had brought her grandson with her. I could tell immediately that it was a setup. They wanted us to meet. He was good-looking in a European way, slightly gray at the temples, with a shy smile like Charles Boyer's. He was obviously a successful businessman who dressed the part. But I was turned off by the idea of a setup, so I cut him dead. I talked only to the two old ladies. Toward the end of the afternoon I realized that he too was annoyed by the obvious ploy and was doing the same thing. He never spoke directly to me or even looked at me. Then I thought, 'Who the devil does he think he is!' I had lived with much more attractive men in Rome. I decided I wanted to go out with him just to teach him a lesson. I did a complete turnaround, gave

him the full treatment, and before we parted, he asked
for a date.

"For the next six months, Gino and I went every-
where together. He wooed me and pursued me with
Italian flair. But I was restless. The more ardent he
became, the more disdainful I was. He kept asking me
to marry him, but my feeling was, Why should I marry
a man with no formal education, no status? Forget it!
Finally, I began to tell him to go away, that I didn't want
to see him anymore. But he wouldn't listen—he was so
persistent!

"One day we had dinner together and went to the
theater; coming home in a taxi, we were caught in a
terrible traffic jam. Once again he asked me to marry
him. In response, I acted badly. I started to scream at
him, 'Get out! Get out of my life!'

"Gino looked at me a long time, and tears welled
up in his eyes. Then he decisively reached out, opened
the door, and stepped out. I watched him weave his way
through the cars. Then I burst into tears. 'I hate him! I
hate him!' I cried.

" 'Doesn't sound that way to me,' the cabbie said
over his shoulder.

"As I sat there in all my misery, I realized the cabbie
was right. What if Gino really left me for good! That was
the catalyst. I finally admitted to myself that I loved him.
He was so wholesome and dear and good, and he
wanted to marry me. I loved him, and I couldn't wait for
that lousy taxi to get me home. Even though it was three
in the morning when I finally reached him, he understood. We've been married for twenty-eight years now
and have terrific kids except for one teenage girl who is
a brat, just like me!"

Love is as volatile as a chemical reaction. It changes things, and it can change people. It can move mountains. We live with it, cope with it, accept it as we are. Then a catalyst comes along and produces reactions that will sometimes astound us. We are in love.

Pause for a moment and think about the married people you know. Why did they ever get married? Do many of them seem mismatched? Some women married men who don't seem to measure up. Some men ended up with wives they could certainly improve upon. What brought them together? What was the catalyst in each case?

Think about your own father and mother, your uncles and aunts, your colleagues at work, your best friends. It is an intriguing game. What were their catalysts? What started it all?

5

"No Chemistry"

From the beginning of civilization to today there have been many more marriages resulting from family arrangement than from romance. The phenomenon of marriage for love is, in fact, a fairly new social custom. In many parts of the world, arranged marriages are still the norm. For hundreds of generations, marriages were arranged by the family, tribe, or monarch. Today the practice is often criticized as uncivilized or primitive, but marriage-by-arrangement persisted for a long time.

I do not advocate a return to marriage by arrangement, but I do think we can learn from some aspects of the past. Many arranged marriages worked because they were rooted in factors that had long-term importance: family, race, religion, society, economics, and survival. They also served to offer very realistic, if not limited, expectations of marriage in the newlyweds. Of course there were disappointments and some mistakes were made. But who can say that there was more unhappiness in arranged marriages than in those that result from our free choice?

The fact is, "free" choice is often based on nothing

more than physical or sexual attraction. This is a weak and limiting foundation on which to build a marriage. When people say, "I felt no chemistry," they mean of course "no sexual chemistry." Alas, how often we judge and write off a potential mate by this single standard.

Sex

Yes, sex can be a powerful catalyst. It whips up the hormones and creates a storm of emotions. Sex is a basic catalyst that ensures our survival as a species—it's primal, primitive, and often overpowering. But it loses its potency with time, like a fragrance or odor that immediately attracts your attention but fades away when you're fully exposed to it for a while. "Chemistry" can be a great catalyst for a one-night stand. And although sexual attraction can be an excellent door opener for a short- or long-term affair, lasting love and marriage require something more.

"No chemistry" is an adolescent judgment, and all too often it is accepted as the final and legitimate verdict by family and friends. It's a nice, safe, socially acceptable answer for rejection.

Incidentally, a negative reaction by men after a first date is usually expressed in some other way than "no chemistry." The reason men don't use it as often may be because of the underlying macho posture that every woman is a potential sexual conquest. (Presumably, if you aren't "turned on" by every woman, you are somewhat less of a man.)

A "no chemistry" report after a first meeting is like a dagger in a matchmaker's heart! I personally find the expression and its easy acceptance as the last word absolutely deplorable. First, it makes sexual attraction the number one priority in assessing a potential spouse. It completely overlooks all other aspirations, goals, needs, and dreams you may have. Is sex the number one priority in your life? Will it be forever?

Second, "no chemistry" often sounds the death knell for any potential romance. It is immediately understood to mean, It's over before it starts; it's hopeless. Is everyone such an expert on sex that they can tell after only one or two dates that there is no adjustment, no communication, no exploration that could result in satisfying sex? As an antidote to this ridiculous view, let me offer an old proverb: The appetite comes with the eating. Did you salivate the first time you saw an olive or an oyster? Didn't you have to taste a new food more than once to decide whether it was a taste you could acquire?

Alas, so many singles allegedly looking for marriage have found "no chemistry" to be a perfect answer for squelching any further dates. This pronouncement has such an air of finality and authority about it, as if it were just a fact of life. Everyone sympathetically understands: "No chemistry—well, forget it. It's nobody's fault, but this duo is a dud!" No further discussion is needed.

What Does "No Chemistry" Really Mean?

Let's take a second look at the "no chemistry" response. First of all, the chemistry of sexual attraction is assumed to have its source in physical appearance. When you say, "He wasn't sexy enough" or "She wasn't pretty enough," you are saying the person didn't measure up to the fantasy created during your childhood and adolescence.

Childhood is when your vision was first formed of what Prince or Princess Charming should look like. As you mature, the fantasy should become a less precise image—that is, if you are really seeing living people and not Disney characters.

But is this the real reason? Often, those making the "no chemistry" judgment after one or two casual meetings may really fear being rejected. They therefore register their rejection first. And the best way to report back to the people who set up the date is to make the rejection something out of your control: "There was no chemistry"—particularly if they suspect, based on fact or just low self-esteem, that their date felt "no chemistry" too.

Others using the excuse simply have come to a premature conclusion and aren't willing to put in the time and energy to see if something can develop in the relationship. They lack patience, so they simply say, "No chemistry."

I say, "baloney!" If you use this ploy, you're cutting yourself off and out. You're leaving the theater before the play has started. Before you decide it's a case of "no chemistry," give it another shot. If the date has any of the characteristics you're looking for—right age, acceptable appearance, a good mind, and so on—then look again. As for being afraid that your date didn't like you, consider that perhaps the person was nervous or under stress and therefore appeared uncomfortable or uninterested. Another meeting at a different time and place may give you both a chance to discover the really wonderful people you are.

By the way, over the years I've learned that men are much more nervous about blind dates than women. This should be a source of comfort to both men and women. To the woman, it is comforting to know that he is even more uptight about this meeting than she is. And as for him, he has the reassurance that there's nothing wrong with him; men generally are nervous on a blind date. So after a first date, remember that he may not have been himself, and she may not have been herself.

If you're not sure—and how can you be?—you must try again. Find out what he or she is really like! Give the engine a chance to start. The motor doesn't always turn over on the first twist of the key.

And, unless the second meeting results in sheer disaster, you should try a third time. If you take your romantic cues solely from the temporary chemistry of sexual attraction, you may never give love a chance to happen.

Recently I had dinner with some old friends, and the conversation got around to my theory of the catalyst factor. I then "guessed" that the woman's husband had met her when they both worked for the same company. With some surprise, she said, "Yes, that's true." I went on to say that the catalyst for him was probably that she was an expert on a certain musical figure—for instance, Mozart. She was thunderstruck, but before she said anything, I added, "At least that's what your husband told me!"

After we had a good laugh, I asked her whether she could recollect what the catalyst was for her. "Well," she said, "I didn't exactly fall in love with him at first sight.

He rushed me that first year, but I had reservations. Richard's not a Casanova, and there were so many other men to meet. But there was a point when my attitude about him changed."

"When was that?"

"When he was sent to an overseas branch for a year, and I started getting his wonderful letters. He wrote the most romantic, witty, engrossing, and heart-warming letters I've ever read. They gave me a new insight into the real Richard. He was not exceptionally articulate in person, but his letters showed the depth of his mind and his decency."

"How long was it before this happened?"

"We knew each other about a year before the letters came. Why do you ask?"

"Well, earlier this evening I asked you how your daughter Amy liked the date I set up for her, and you told me that she thought he was a nice young man, intelligent and attractive, but there was no chemistry, and she probably would not go out with him again. Isn't she missing the chance to find out whether he can write wonderful letters?"

Love Is a Building Process

Love is slower and more deliberate than the fireworks of infatuation. It's more like building your own home. There must be plans for the future, built on a reasonable foundation. You add tier by tier with affection and attention to detail. The wondrous aspect is that two unique human beings are meshed. The pull and push, the action and reaction, enable love to materialize.

How often did the classmate or fellow employee that you couldn't stand at first later become your best friend? How sad it would be if you had cut your friend off after a first meeting with a verdict of "no chemistry."

6

The Dumper/Dumpee Syndrome

One of the biggest single deterrents to establishing a relationship is a syndrome that prevents people from giving the catalyst time to work its magic. Highly eligible people who have every reason to be popular and who very much want to be married never connect. Why? Often because they're victims of what I call the Dumper/Dumpee Syndrome. This may not be the most elegant language with which to describe what I mean, but over the years I've found that everyone understands immediately what I'm trying to convey. Just to be sure, let me explain.

It comes about like this. A man who gets dumped may shrug it off the first time, but when it happens again, he becomes gun-shy. If it happens several times, he may become badly scarred and dread the thought of being rejected again. So in order to avoid being the *dumpee,* he jumps to being the *dumper.* He spends years shopping and dating without having any kind of deep, lasting relationship. His reaction after a first date is "She's kind of nice, but I've got to have someone special." If the dumper is a woman, she's apt to say, "He's too weak," or too passive, too ambitious, too short, too tall, and so on.

This Dumper/Dumpee Syndrome nips romance before it gets a chance to bud for either the man or the woman. Early rejectors don't give the catalyst enough time to work; they just ditch whatever budding relationship might develop to avoid possible future heartbreak. I've seen it over and over again in both men and women.

Some years ago I arranged a blind date for my friend Ralph. His wife had left him for another man, and he had been deeply hurt. The woman was an attorney too, and they had much in common. Both were intelligent, charming, and successful but lonely, childless, and middle-aged. They went to dinner and a Broadway show. Ralph had spared no expense, but it had not ended well. He called the next day to thank me and report, "She's nice enough, intelligent, with an attractive face, but she does have rather heavy legs . . . not for me. I need someone really special."

I met her later that week. She was bubbling with enthusiasm and gratitude. "He's such a great guy. I really like him. I just can't wait to go out with him again."

"Oh, how do you think the evening went?"

"I thought we were both having a great time right up to the end, then he kind of switched. Is he very moody?"

"Not that I've noticed," I responded. "But did he ask you out again?"

"Well, yes, as we got close to my apartment, he asked me whether I was free next Saturday night, and I said, 'Sorry, I'm busy.' In retrospect that was the turning point; from then on he got glum. Polite, of course, but rather removed. Do you think maybe I should have said, 'Sorry, I'm busy Saturday night, but I'd love to go out with you on Friday or Sunday'?"

"Yes, I do. You triggered his defense mechanism and made him into a 'dumper'!"

But all was not lost. She called him—much to his surprise and delight—and they arranged for another date. They're now "steadies."

Sonia and Maggie are cousins and have been inseparable friends from childhood. Maggie is very attractive, athletic, and full of fun. Sonia is somewhat plain and very sensible but definitely in Maggie's shadow when they are together. Maggie's looks and personality attracted many dates for the two of them. It was always quite apparent that the men were interested in Maggie and accepted Sonia as part of the package. It was therefore rather ironic that Sonia was the more picky of the two. There was rarely, if ever, a date that Sonia liked, and she was deadly in uncovering some weakness or fault in the man who was unlucky enough to take her out.

Then one day, Maggie got married, and Sonia began to go out alone, with rather strange and unpredictable results. She actually enjoyed the company of men. Now there was no need to reject her date before he showed a preference for someone else. She was able to relax and savor her partners, and they in turn had a chance to appreciate her.

Not long after Maggie's marriage, Sonia met a man and fell in love. He would never have survived the old Sonia.

Sonia was a classic product of the Dumper/Dumpee Syndrome. As an adolescent and young woman she was constantly reminded, by the way boys and men flocked to Maggie, that she was a second choice. So she began to reject men before they could reject her, with predictable results. Even a star is overlooked in the presence of a full moon.

This case history highlights another important lesson. Many of us, both men and women, feel uptight about going out alone. We're comfortable only when we have the security of a friend with us. This can be a serious mistake because we never act the same when there is a third or fourth person present. Love and marriage is a one-on-one experience; other people only muddy the water! An audience turns us into actors, and we're looking for the real thing, not a performance.

How to Break the Syndrome

If you suffer from this syndrome, the way to cope with it is to face up to it and recognize how harmful and self-defeating it is. Force yourself to try for a second date. Resolve never to make up your mind until after the third meeting. Yes, you may waste some time, but at least you won't be casting aside an unopened gift.

Even those of us who do not suffer from the extreme form of the Dumper/Dumpee Syndrome tend to back off and hide our true emotions. When single people meet for the first time, the paramount question, conscious or not, is, does he or she like me? In the interests of harmony and personal security, we have all learned to mask what we feel. For example, it's most unusual that we'd let anyone in a business or social context know that we dislike them. Even if we think them rude, uncouth, dull, stupid, or boring, we will probably treat them in a bland, casual, almost friendly way.

If, on the other hand, we meet someone for the first time and really like them—find them interesting or stimulating or fun to talk to—we also tend to treat them in a bland, casual, and friendly way. Why? Because part of the civilizing process conditions us to hide our feelings. We've learned to restrain ourselves from being too open. The result is it's very hard to know for sure how people feel about us.

This is doubly true in a situation where you've just met an eligible single. There's immediate anxiety and pressure. "Do I like her? I don't know, it depends—does she like me?" "If he likes me, maybe I do like him." And so on. Thus, after the first date or so, there is always some ambivalence. The jury is still out.

There are two challenges presented by the Dumper/Dumpee Syndrome. The first challenge is when you yourself have become a dumper because you so dread being rejected. The way to tackle this is to take stock of yourself and come to the conclusion that you're a pretty nice person, that your appearance and accomplishments are fine, that you have many friends and family that like you and think you're great. Then if someone you just met doesn't seem to like you, it's really a reflection on that person. Having a good sense of self-worth is a strong bulwark against the trauma of being dumped. When you've licked the fear of being rejected, you won't fall into the knee-jerk pattern of rejecting potential partners on the first date.

The second challenge is how to cope with a rejector you're meeting on a first date. Now that you understand how a rejector gets that way, it's easy. The rejector acts out of fear, out of an imagined need for self-defense. You can nullify that fear by making it absolutely clear that you like the person, that you find him or her interesting, and that you want to go out again. It's hard to reject someone you've just met who obviously is taken with you.

It's not unusual for both parties on a blind date to be dumpers. Rejectors always need new people, new blind dates. They rarely establish a relationship because the terrible need to reject first makes it all but impossible! They are nevertheless driven by the human hunger for friendship and must look for someone.

Be honest—are you a dumper? Do you manage to get the first punch in? Do you have one foot pointed the other way—ready to run away the moment you meet someone new?

As a matchmaker, this is when I've been of some help. In the majority of cases, when I ask either of the parties about the date and get a reserved, hesitant answer, I know the romance is still possible. In that case, I never hesitate to say that the other person liked him or her—and I'm telling the truth! It's only when one person actually dislikes the other that I get a strong, direct response, such as "He's a nice person but he's definitely not my type." Then I know for certain the date was a bomb.

But what happens when there's no third party to supply the reassuring feedback and the Dumper/Dumpee Syndrome goes into action? That's when you need the "Big Hello," described in the next chapter.

7

The Big Hello

Many years ago a young girl came to work in our law office as a file clerk and general "gofer." I say *girl* because of her thin, waiflike appearance, although she must have been twenty or twenty-one at the time. Despite her look of shyness, she was cheerful, intelligent, and very energetic. I was much impressed with her, but I wondered why she never said hello or good-bye.

She worked part-time and would suddenly appear in the morning or afternoon, when you noticed her doing some of her chores. Her departures were like that too. She'd just disappear like a wisp of smoke. "She was just filing those papers. Now where is she?"

One day I asked her, "Betty, why is it you never say hello or good-bye?"

"Oh, Mr. Fisher, I do."

"I've never heard you."

"Well, I used to say it louder, but no one ever responded. I couldn't tell for sure whether they were ignoring me or just didn't hear me. Maybe they thought I wasn't important enough. So gradually I just started saying it to myself."

"Why, Betty, of course I'd say hello to you if you greeted me."

"I'm glad to hear that! I sort of didn't want to rock the boat."

"Betty, Betty, what a silly way to solve the problem. And it's a problem we all face. How do people feel about us? Are they friends or enemies? What we say and how we act is shaped by whom we're with. We're guarded with enemies, open with friends. Rather than risk being snubbed, you tried to become invisible, appearing and disappearing without drawing attention to yourself. And you partially succeeded: nobody snubs you, but nobody knows you're alive. Surely that's not what you want."

"But if I draw attention to myself, maybe some of the people won't like me."

"So what? We can't expect everyone to like us. The important thing is to have a sense of how people feel about us. You need to know who likes you and who doesn't like you so that you can act accordingly."

"But how can I find out?"

"Try using the 'Big Hello.' Here's what I mean.

"When you enter a room and join a group of people, give them a big hello. Say it loud enough so that there's no doubt as to whether anyone heard you or not. Now, if someone ignores you or snubs you, there'll be no question that it's intentional. And you'll know how to act toward him or her in the future. On the other hand, you'll probably get a big hello back from some of the others, and you'll be reassured about how they feel about you too."

Making the First Move

To illustrate the Big Hello, let me tell you another tale from my matchmaking files.

Very old and dear friends told me about someone they knew, a single woman in her early thirties who was anxious to get married.

Would I help? Feeling somewhat ornery at the time, I said I was so overwhelmed with matchmaking tasks, I wasn't taking the names of any more singles. I also added that I could not help anyone I didn't know personally or hadn't at least met. After all, it was an avocation, not a dating service!

My friends were disappointed. But three days later I got a telephone call from Audrey, who identified herself as the single woman in question. I was intrigued by her spunk when she said, "Where, how, and when can we meet?" Instead of responding to her question, I gave her a half-hour phone interview, during which I posed searching questions, and I was impressed by her answers. She was a bit rigid, but also intelligent and charming, and determined to find a husband.

I finally said, "OK, Audrey, I'm putting you in my 'computer,' but you're going to have to overcome a series of hurdles."

"I'm ready. What do I have to do?"

"I'm going to give you the name and telephone number of a young man who lives in Virginia. Call him up and tell him I suggested that you have a lot in common."

"I could never do that! Why, I've never called a man

I didn't know. And in Virginia! I live in New York. What's the point?"

"It looks like you've failed the first hurdle."

"What's the second one?"

"To report on what happened on the first hurdle."

"You want me to change my whole way of acting. I'd never make the first call, and I surely would never report to anyone what happened—that's private. I have standards!"

"Perhaps you should ask yourself, 'How am I doing?' Maybe it's time you took a second look at your standards."

After a long pause, she said, "OK, I give up. What's his name and number?"

Two days later Steven, the Virginian, called me. He told me with some excitement, "We spoke for almost an hour, and she seems like a very interesting woman. I'm coming up to New York on Memorial Day, and we have a date."

Next day, I got a call from Audrey. She too was enthusiastic. But she added, "I hated the idea of making that first call. Why couldn't he call me first?"

"Well, what happened when you called?"

"Nothing. We made a date."

"Enough said. Call me with a report after your date."

After Memorial Day, Steven met me in New York before returning home. He said, "She's quite good-looking, really a very lovely woman. We spent about five hours together, going to an art show and having a leisurely dinner. It was a pleasant evening."

"Will you try to see her again?"

"No. Frankly, I don't think she found me very

interesting. There were a lot of long pauses in our conversation, and when we said good night, she seemed rather distant. But don't be afraid to set up a date for her with another guy. She's OK."

A few days later Audrey called and wanted to know whether I'd heard from Steven.

"First," I said, "what did you think of him?"

"He's terrific. You said he was a bit short. He's not; he's perfect. I liked everything about him."

"Did you let him know that you liked him?"

"Well . . . no."

"Do you want to see him again?"

"Yes!"

"But you didn't tell him that?"

"Of course not. I'm not going to throw myself at a man. But tell me, what did he say? Is he going to take me out again?"

"I don't think so. He said you were very attractive and lovely, but he didn't think you liked him."

"But that's terrible! I liked him very much."

What a sad tale—and one that happens again and again. In personal, one-on-one relationships, how people feel about us is what we care about. The greatest stumbling block to romance is the fear of indifference by the other party. But somebody's got to take the first step, so when it comes to wanting someone to like you, use the Big Hello. Let people know you like them. You'll get an instant reaction. If the feeling is mutual, then romance can flower. If your feelings are not reciprocated, then you'll know right away, free from any ambivalence. But even more, the Big Hello is a great catalyst. When people know you like them, they tend to respond generously. They like you in return. It's just that simple.

Back to Audrey and Steven. While Audrey was bemoaning the fate of her relationship with Steven, I told her she had another hurdle to try: "Call him up and tell him what a lovely time you had and that you want to see him again."

She groaned. "I can't do that!"

"OK. Forget it. Some day your Prince Charming will come along on his white horse and sweep you right out of your living room. So all you have to do is wait."

She sighed. "All right. I'll try."

She called a day later. She and Steven made another date for the Fourth of July weekend. We'll see what happens if they can keep up the momentum.

The point I want to drive home is that you must do something! Enough of the Sleeping Beauty approach! You can't just snooze your way to romance. Even in that fairy tale, one of the parties had to *do* something. The prince kissed her. He woke her up; he broke the spell. But it could have been the other way around: she could have kissed him. In real life, often the most eligible bachelors are asleep, waiting for a princess to awaken them from their slumber.

The high point in Marty's change from withdrawn widower to available bachelor came about as follows. He had just started to go out again, but a highly touted blind date proved to be only a so-so evening. She was attractive, the right age, and so on, but during the three hours they spent together, it was clear they had different goals and agendas. She wanted to find someone rich and retired so that they could spend the rest of their lives as members of a country club set, traveling around the world and wintering in Palm Beach. Marty was looking for a woman who had a life of her own and career goals he might help her achieve.

Nevertheless, the blind date had a pleasant aftermath. About two weeks later, Marty got a lovely invitation to a party in New York, with a personal note from the hostess. The note said that her friend (the former date) had given her Marty's name, and she looked forward to meeting him. The day arrived, and he was quite excited—his first party in his new life. As he entered the very posh building, the doorman gave him a big smile and said Apartment 7B. The door was open when he got there—wall-to-wall people. Music and happy conversation floated above the crowd. Marty edged his way in, and an attractive, well-dressed woman introduced herself as the hostess. "I'm so happy you could come. I've been dying to meet you. Why don't you mingle for a while? I have to welcome some other guests."

The two-and-a-half-room apartment was packed. There were thirty men and exactly twelve women. A fabulous party for the bachelorettes who had planned it. Despite the imbalance, he had a good time talking to many of the men. Their ages ranged from the twenties to the seventies. The women all seemed to be in their thirties. As one of the few men courageous enough to dance, Marty eventually met all of the women. But none of them, including the hostess, seemed right for him.

Since he had a long trip home, he started to leave early. As he worked his way toward the door, the hostess took his hand and joined him. She walked him to the elevator as he explained the reason for the early departure. She said, "I'm so sorry you're going, but thanks for coming and livening up the party." Then she put her arms around him and gave him a lusty kiss on the lips. Marty was startled and somewhat dumbstruck. "We had barely met!" he told me later. The elevator door opened, and as he backed into it she wagged her finger and added, "Don't forget you owe me one!" Marty's head was in a whirl. Did she mean a kiss or a date?

That was a Big Hello and it worked. Marty dated her within a week.

I do not necessarily advocate grabbing a man and kissing him on your first meeting. This is, however, a rather dramatic example of the Big Hello and how it works. She got his attention, woke him up, and converted Marty from a disinterested spectator to an active player.

The Big Hello takes many forms and guises, and it should fit your personality and style. But above all, it should get the message across to him or her: "I like you. I want more!"

How to Personalize the Big Hello

Now here's a little exercise to personalize the Big Hello that will help you develop your own Big Hello. Make a list of twenty-five ways you can show someone you like him or her. (Actually, there are hundreds of ways!) Keep working on it until you've got twenty-five ways that you like—a Big Hello for him or her. It helps if you have a specific person in mind. If you can't do it all right now, start the list on a piece of paper and keep adding to it until there are twenty-five. Tape the list to your bath-room mirror so that you can see it and maybe add to it every morning. If you want to go for fifty, that's even better. Once you begin to work on the Big Hello seri-ously, you'll find that you've added it to your lifestyle and you'll be astounded with the results.

Here are a few obvious examples:

1. A friendly smile whenever you meet.
2. Close attention. Be a good listener.
3. Compliments on clothing or appearance.
4. Help in work or play without being asked.
5. Laughing at his jokes.
6. Bringing a flower or a pizza or a cold Coke.
7. Holding the door.
8. Waiting for him.
9. Walking with her.
10. Sending a letter.

Your first reaction may be to scoff at these exam-ples, but the tiny, inconsequential items of life are the small change of interpersonal relations. They aid and stimulate the flow of communication and under-standing. Most of all, they open up the channel for important messages to follow, like "I want you," "I love you."

8

Learn to Love the Possible

At some point in your life, you awake to find that the romantic dream you've pursued for lo these many years will probably not materialize. The prince or princess you've been waiting for lives in the same never-never land as Santa Claus and the Tooth Fairy. But that's not the end of the world. In fact, this awakening may be only the beginning for you! You may finally decide: "I really want to get married!" rather than: "I'll get married when and if certain conditions are met."

It's like going to college. When you are determined to get a college education, you'll find a college that will take you, and you'll do the work you need to get in. The college may not be the one your friends all talked about or the one featured in the movies or on television. It may not have a championship football team, the most beautiful and fun-loving students, or famous professors. But if you really want an education, you'll make the adjustments necessary to get in. You'll go to an out-of-town or out-of-state school, or to an inner-city school, or to a school with no campus, no teams, no glamour, no hoopla. All of these are mere icing on the cake and should not be confused with your basic goal of a college education.

When you have an important goal, don't be side-tracked by hurdles and bumps in the road. Keep your eye on the target and go for it. If the joys of marriage are what you want, there are potential partners waiting for you!

This analogy is best summed up by Bonnie, a brilliant and attractive woman who confided her tale to me.

"At thirty-five I wanted to be married, not just married to a certain someone that fit an image in my mind, but in the 'state of married.' And so I looked for someone who would enable me to live and be happy in that condition—married! Most single people run around looking for the one they'd like to marry, not for the one they can be married with.

"I've been married eight years now, and we're very happy. Some of my friends don't think he's a great bargain, but he's my husband and I'm his wife. He gives me the things I need: friendship, caring and sharing, moral and emotional support (I supply my own financial support). I trust him and he trusts me. He's someone I can help, too, and I enjoy helping him. He enables me to participate in the experience of being married. That's what I wanted and that's what I got!"

Looking for Marilyn

I once got an important insight into the pursuit of romantic happiness from a totally unrelated source. I have a friend who is an attorney, a single practitioner who grinds out all his legal papers himself. He's overwhelmed with details and deadlines, so his secretary is even more important and involved than most legal secretaries. For the past several years whenever we had lunch, Tom would bemoan the fact that his current secretary was (1) efficient but dull, (2) friendly but a goof-off, (3) stupid, (4) conscientious but a terrible slob, (5) hardworking but with no skills, and (6) not like Marilyn.

Marilyn had been his loyal and efficient secretary in the early years when he was building his practice. She had retired after twenty years with him. Tom never recovered from her departure, and he compared every secretary to her. He was always complaining that there was no one like Marilyn, there never would be, et cetera, et cetera.

Finally I said, "Why don't you wake up? You've changed. You're more demanding, more rigid, and less tolerant. I bet if a Marilyn clone started to work for you today, you'd find something wrong with her. You've got to learn to love the possible! Stop trying to find a figment of your remembered past. Accept what's real and available and learn to love it."

He must have listened. He's had the same secretary now for three years, and his secretarial problems are no longer part of our weekly luncheon discussions.

The Art of the Possible

Recently, my wife, Carol, and I attended a large and joyous family party. Among the many friends and relatives was a young woman of about twenty-five. She was attractive, albeit rather world-weary for one so young. The conversation soon turned to my matchmaking, and I asked her what kind of man she would find interesting. She acted as though the conversation was objectionable as well as infinitely boring, but she promptly advised me she never went out with anyone under six feet tall. When I said I knew a young attorney that would fill the bill, she wanted to know what kind of practice he had. I told her he worked in the Public Defender's office, protecting the rights of abused welfare children.

"Oh, no," she said, with some disdain. "I would never go out with a *social worker.*"

Later her mother confided to me, "It's a funny thing—she's such a beautiful girl and has so much going for her, but men don't flock to her."

Small wonder. I guess it's their instinct for survival.

I'm sure this young lady thinks that her rigid attitude is vital for her happiness. But from my point of view, it does nothing but cut her off from the adventure of life. She'd be happier if she'd learn to love the possible.

Does this mean giving up things that matter deeply to you? Not at all. There will always be one or several qualities that you regard as absolutely essential in a spouse, your sine qua non, the essential element or condition you shouldn't live without. What is your sine qua non? Somebody who likes to spend vacations hiking in the woods? Somebody who has a sense of humor? Somebody who loves living in the city? Somebody who wants to have children? Learning to love the possible doesn't mean settling for less than the essential.

It does mean opening up new possibilities. How many women are looking for a short, bald man with a slight paunch? Yet there are probably thousands of bald, paunchy bachelors floating around who are also warm, sensitive, compassionate, and fun to be with—potentially great husbands and fathers, just waiting to be noticed. How many men would say they're looking for a tall, skinny, bespectacled, bookish woman? But there are probably hundreds whose wit and good humor, given half the chance, would charm a man's socks off.

We often write scenarios of romantic happiness for a production taking place in our heads. We audition and select the Prince Charming or the damsel-in-distress, design the victories and defeats, develop the heroes and the villains. This being so, why not create fantasies that can happen, daydreams that are possible, rather than scenarios that can never happen? Those who obsessively yearn for a chance encounter with a movie star, which will suddenly thrust them into a glamorous, jet-set life, are doing themselves an injustice. They are robbing themselves of opportunities to find the real happiness that may lie within their reach. By concentrating on capturing the pie in the sky, they prevent themselves from achieving those joys and treasures actually available.

Here's an example: Rhoda is only a year older than her sister Hazel. They have always been rivals. Rhoda was a brilliant student, got all A's; she was a cheerleader; she got a scholarship to college and later to graduate school. Hazel, on the other hand, was a so-so student. Easygoing and congenial, she married the most eligible bachelor in town. She now lives in a large house in the most fashionable suburb.

At thirty, Rhoda is well into her career in banking. She is unmarried and unhappy about it. She says there is no one around for her. Her standards are very high, and she feels she could never accept anyone less accomplished than she. To make her terms even more impossible, she compares everyone to Hazel's rich and handsome husband. Why shouldn't she get a man like that?

Why, indeed! Well, Rhoda doesn't realize that her ability and high motivation, which made her such a success in school and business, frighten many of the ever smaller pool of candidates still around. Also, many of the men who are strong, highly motivated, and successful don't want a competitor for a wife.

Does this mean there is no romantic future for Rhoda? Not at all! She can dream and search as long as she wants; it could happen. But at some point in her life she must turn from the all-but-impossible and concentrate on the possible.

Instead of looking only for a man she considers superior to her, she should concentrate on finding a man who will appreciate her, recognize her ability, and be proud of her accomplishments, a man who wants to give love to her and accept love from her.

Reassessing Your Criteria

Understanding where we got our expectations helps us assess them. One important source of criteria is your family. Perhaps you have witnessed this scene either live or on television: It's the moment of high drama at a wedding, and all of the principals have appeared and taken their places. There is a hush of expectation; the musicians strike up the joyous, triumphant "Here Comes the Bride," and the beautiful bride (all brides are beautiful) is ushered down the aisle by her father or both her parents or some representative of her family. But at the end of the aisle, the bridegroom joins her. Then together they stand alone at the altar.

The important message here is that your parents can take you only so far. At some point, you must go on without them. But never underestimate the importance of your family's imprint on you. It's indelible! All of the education and all of the therapy and all of the soap in the world cannot wash it out. But there comes a time when you and you alone must decide what is essential in your life and in your lifelong partner; what changes and choices you must make, regardless of whether your choices are in accord with those of your mother, father, sister, brother, or favorite aunt.

Often it's our social environment that influences and shapes our criteria. Like teenagers in a gang, we want to be different and at the same time similar to everyone else in the gang. We're afraid of deviating too much from the norm, so we set up the same criteria as everyone else in our crowd. Thus, we narrow the group of possible choices and make the search harder and more competitive.

Sometimes people fail to reassess or update their changing needs as they get older. They stick to obsolete goals, holding onto criteria that are no longer important or necessary.

For example, if you're in your forties or fifties or older, surely there are things more important to you than the way someone looks. Yet because there was a time when you thought "he must be cute" or "she must be beautiful," you keep looking for someone who is cute or beautiful. You've conditioned yourself that way.

However, as time passes, what you thought was vital yesterday becomes less important today. You begin to reassess the things you thought you wanted. This reassessment actually helps you in your search because if you're really ready to get married, you'll get down to basics and concentrate on them. And basics are so much easier to find than the frills and fantasies.

Don't think you have to settle for less just because you're older. As we get older, we can choose for ourselves more wisely. If you've found yourself in several unhappy or dead-end relationships, now is the time to reconsider your criteria. Take the case of David, a freelance journalist in his middle thirties. David told me: "A few years ago, before I met my wife, everybody I got involved with turned out to be wrong for me. My relationships weren't too healthy and never went anywhere. So I decided to deliberately select a new set of criteria. I asked myself, What do I really want in a partner? Then I began looking for these things. Not everybody would want to use my criteria, but they worked for me." What were they, I wanted to know.

"Well, first of all, I wanted a woman who liked her work and was happy in her life. Next, I didn't want to be involved with another journalist—too much competition in one household. Finally, I wanted somebody who really enjoyed sex." Note that David's criteria didn't have anything to do with looks, brains, or status. He was practical and realistic. He could really use his criteria to exclude women who were wrong for him and identify those that might make him happy. He's been happily married now for five years and describes his relationship with his wife in one word: "Great!"

The Alternative

This may be as good a place as any to discuss why it's important to learn to love the possible. Consider the alternative! It's like the great choice given by a mugger when he says, "Your wallet or your life." It helps you make up your mind quickly.

The alternative to getting married is staying single. There are many people who insist that they prefer to remain single, and they surely have every right to make that choice. But for many, the single life can be bleak and lonely, destined to be barren of the friendship, intimacies, and richness of experience that marriage and a family can bring.

The single life can be made to seem very glamorous, exciting, and even heroic during your younger years, but as time wears you down, the glamour becomes a hollow mask.

In 1900, the life expectancy at birth in the United States was forty-nine years; in 1991, it was seventy-one for men and seventy-eight for women. Any number of studies show that married men live longer than single men. This is true for happily married women, too. In any event the quality of married life promises more for couples in their middle and senior years. Loving and sharing with a best friend becomes more important as the scenario of your life unfolds.

I remember a terribly depressing story I heard many years ago when I was vacationing in Miami. Sitting by the pool at dusk, I was chatting with an attractive middle-aged woman who must have been even more beautiful in her youth. When I learned she was single, I remarked, "I'm surprised that a woman with all your charms hasn't been married."

Sadly, she told me her story. "Oh, I was pretty good-looking when I was young, and I had plenty of chances. I started to work as a typist for a large corporation and kept getting promoted. So I went to school at night to become better qualified. Eventually, I became executive assistant to the president. I made a very good salary, and I still do, but I was too busy to go out much. My family were immigrants, and they were unhappy about my life. Everyone was saying, 'When is she going to get married? What's wrong with her? Is she too good for everybody?' and remarks like that. It got to me, and I began to look around. Most of the single men in the company were third-generation Americans. While they made passes at me, they weren't serious, and there was no future with them. So I started to date some of the men in my family's social circle. They were immigrants or first-generation Americans like me.

"There was one man who was just crazy about me, and after a few months he asked me to marry him. He was very handsome and loving, came from a good family and so on, but he was only a butcher. Actually, I was making more money than he at that time. It was a tough decision. Finally, I decided yes. He was overjoyed, and we set a date to pick out a ring. At the jewelers they showed us dozens of rings, and I had no trouble picking out the one I wanted. It was pretty big and very beautiful. He got very quiet and said, 'I can't afford that,' and pointed instead to a smaller one. I got angry and said, 'Absolutely not!' And that was that; the whole engagement was off. You know it wasn't only the ring—I began to see my whole future, living in a lousy three-room apartment, struggling to make it, on the edge of poverty just like my parents. The funny part of the story is that he married a cousin of mine. They have three children, and he has his own butcher shop in Manhattan now."

"Well, how do you feel about it today?" I asked.

"I was stupid. He was basically a good man, and I could have made something of him. He was crazy about me, and we could have had a good life together, but I guess I was too young and had a cockeyed sense of values!"

Another friend who was quite successful and came from a very wealthy family was fond of accounting for his family's prosperity by saying, "Oh, my folks were among the early settlers."

I knew that his was the first generation born in

America, and so I was puzzled. Finally I said, "Gerry, what's this business about your folks being among the early settlers? They only got to America about fifty years ago."

"You're so right, but you misunderstand me. When I say 'early settlors,' spelled with an *o*, I'm referring to business deals. In every business transaction there's some negotiation—some back and forth, some give and take until a deal is struck. My folks never held out for the best deal. Once they saw a fair offer, they settled and closed the deal. I'm an early settlor too. I never try to hold out for the last drop of blood."

What does that story have to do with you? It's an object lesson. I'm not suggesting that you settle for less than you deserve, but I do suggest you see things as they really are. Do not set your heart on some fantasy that can never become part of your reality.

The Wish List

Make a wish list of the things important to you in a potential spouse. Let your mind go, fantasize and explore how you feel, and include everything you've ever been concerned about. In addition to the criteria mentioned so far, also list tiny details that you might never mention to anyone else but that are nevertheless important to you: clean nails, long legs, beautiful lips, a generous laugh, fashionable clothes, a refined manner. Don't stop until you have a list of at least twenty items; it could be thirty or even fifty.

Now look at the list. Go over each item and ask yourself, "How important is that? Is this one a standard a prospective spouse must meet, or can this be eliminated? Does it go to the very essence of my needs?"

For example, if you were very religious, you might feel that you could never marry anyone who was not of your faith. Put a number alongside each item on your list: 1) for those characteristics that are absolutely all-important, 2) for those that are sort of important, and 3) for those that are not really important at all.

Now go over your list of 1's and ask yourself, "Why?" For example, a woman might write, "He must be taller than I." Why? "Well, we'd look ridiculous if I married a shrimp." Are you saying that how a couple looks makes for the success or failure of a marriage? "No, of course not, but I would like him to be taller."

Suppose he were ideal in every other way, would you let four or six or even twelve inches stand between you and happiness? "Oh, I don't know." Then his height should not be a 1; maybe a 2, but surely not a 1. "OK, it's a 2."

Go over your list aggressively, honestly, and see how many items are still number-one priorities. This exercise is vitally important because there are potential spouses in your past that on a subliminal level you rejected as "not possible," based on criteria you thought of as 1's. Now they are only 2's, or even 3's. Go through your memory and salvage what you can, but in any event move ahead with a more open mind.

Loving the Possible

People who have "learned to love the possible" are all around you. All you have to do is look and think about it. There are few marriages indeed where the bride or groom exactly fits the other's dream. But that's no impediment to their happiness. They each overlook the inconsequential imperfections or shortfalls and concentrate on what the marriage will mean for them.

This concept was so much better understood by our grandparents or parents who were new to America and by people who lived through the Depression. They had a sense that they had to get on with life, that there was a time for sowing and a time for reaping, that they had to make the best of things: Loving the possible was not bad.

I recall one very happy marriage in which tremendous adjustments were made by both the husband and wife because they were mature enough to embrace what was possible and ignore what others thought—indeed, what they had thought—when they were younger. She was a professor at a prominent university, renowned for her research and writing. She had been married and widowed for several years and was now facing a rather lonely life despite her zest for living.

He was from South Africa, a self-made man who had made a fortune manufacturing alligator bags. He had started working in his teens and had never finished high school. At mid-life he divorced his wife to end an unhappy marriage and came to the United States to start over. Alone in America, with no friends or relatives, he had a great hunger for intellectual pursuits.

They met at a concert on the college campus. An unlikely couple to be sure. She was at least ten years older than he, all elegance and style; he was somewhat shorter, unpolished, and foreign to the ways of her world.

She had never dreamed that she'd accept anyone with less than two degrees, and he would have been appalled at the thought of marrying someone only eight years younger than his mother.

Nevertheless, within four months they had become best friends and eventually realized that they'd be happier married. It's now seven years since they acted on the possible!

Recently, my wife's friend Heather chided me for not introducing her to "really great guys like Allen," who was sitting on the other side of the room with his fiancée. I was shocked for a moment. Then I realized she was serious and sadly responded, "But, Heather, I introduced you to him several years ago at our housewarming!"

"You're kidding. I never saw him before."

"Don't you remember the man who walked you out to your car in the rain?"

"Sure I do—but that guy wore glasses, and I never was attracted to men with glasses."

Heather's antipathy to glasses cost her. She never got the opportunity to really know Allen or to see him later with his contact lenses. Her narrow, self-imposed standards cut her choices and opportunities.

In the above example, on a subliminal level, Heather wiped out perfectly appropriate candidates because they failed to meet some standard that to a mature adult is little more than fluff.

We all have a tendency to hold onto likes and dislikes long after there is any reason for them. We're like Linus in the "Peanuts" comic strip, still holding onto our baby blanket. So reconsider your criteria list;

check it and revise it periodically. If you hold onto adolescent expectations long after you've outgrown them, you may find yourself growing old alone.

My friend Ian called me the other day to talk of a breakthrough. He's a very shy young man in his mid-thirties who has been dating for years, but he "never seems to find the right kind of girl." I suspect many women were turned off by his diffident manner. During the past few months, he's grown up. I say this because he has made some radical attitude changes in the kind of girl he would take out. For years his admonition to me has been "no fat girls, I can't stand fat ankles." This time our conversation went like this. "Well, I finally met her. She's a definite finalist."

"Hurrah, what happened?"

"I went to a dance Sunday night, and it was the usual thing. People kept pairing off and sticking to each other. I danced a few times, but no one gave me any encouragement. Then when there was only about fifteen minutes left in the evening, a fairly attractive woman came over and asked me to dance. She was fun, full of spunk, and very upbeat. She was a little plump, but her dancing was great. Before I knew it, the dance was over and we had to split. But I set up a date for next Saturday. And you know what: She told me we had met years ago and that she had kind of a crush on me, but I never gave her a tumble. I do remember the party where she said we met, but I absolutely don't remember her. Maybe she was fatter in those days."

Maybe she was, but maybe Ian's eyesight was narrower then too.

Thank goodness, we have the ability to change and modify the standards we impose on ourselves.

The Guided Dream Fantasy

Here is an exercise I use in class to enable students to find answers and insight from within. In a guided dream fantasy, we set up a scenario and environment and allow participants to continue to visualize or fantasize a conclusion on their own. It has special advantages since it's created by the dreamer, observed only by him, and does not have to be disclosed. Very often the revelations uncovered by the dreamers have profound effects on their lives and attitudes.

Try it. This little experiment may help you realize what is really important in the mate you're looking for. This guided dream is set up for a woman, but you can easily adjust it to be used by a man.

Imagine this:

You are on an airplane, flying off to a kind of Club Med vacation. The plane is filled with people like yourself, all within a fifteen- to twenty-year age span, all eagerly looking forward to a much dreamed of vacation. As you look around the plane and size up the men, you make mental notes and find yourself getting depressed. The two in the first row are too short. The next three rows are filled with members of an ethnic group you're definitely not interested in. In the middle section of the plane the men are too loud, badly dressed, have terrible teeth, and are either too fat or bald.

There are one or two interesting looking men toward the rear of the plane, but they seem to be very involved with the girls they are seated with. So it's easy to understand why you are feeling deflated. The only thing that perks you up a little is the thought that there are sure to be other men at the hotel, maybe someone who will meet your standards.

Suddenly, all of the lights go out on the plane and the pilot's voice comes over the PA system, telling the passengers to remain calm and fasten their seat belts. In a few minutes, the pilot manages a bumpy landing on the water and urges everyone to remain calm and abandon the plane.

The next thing you remember is reaching consciousness on the floor of an inflated rubber raft and hearing the gentle lapping of the waves against the sides. As you pull yourself together and look around at the vast stretch of empty water, you become aware of a body lying on the other side of the raft. It's a man, unconscious, bleeding from a cut on the side of his head. You prop him up and try to bring him back to consciousness by washing his face with seawater and gently slapping it. Fortunately, there's an emergency kit on the raft, and you are able to stop the bleeding and bandage his wound. A shot of whiskey brings him around; then he opens his eyes and asks, "Where am I?"

You realize at once that he's one of the men you rejected on the plane. It's hard to remember why because the accident has confused you. But you do remember that he was totally unacceptable.

You're not sure how long you drift in that desolate sea, but you talk for hours and are silent for hours. You're very grateful when he lies down beside you during that long cold night. The warmth of his body and his gentle reassuring breathing help you to finally get to sleep.

What joy to find at dawn that the raft has washed ashore on a tropical island. In the days and weeks that follow, you find that it is a small island. About three days of walking take you from one end to the other. There is ample fresh water, fruit, nuts, vegetables, fresh seafood, and various small game. There are trees and grass and colorful fragrant flowers——but no other human beings.

Joe, for that is your companion's name, has many characteristics you don't like. He's a little heavy and he's shorter than you. He's a college dropout who now works as a chef in a large hotel. He's a little rough around the edges but good-natured, with plenty of street smarts. He pitches in cheerfully. You see that he has a quick intelligence; he can size up every situation and decide how to cope with it. He is gentle and supportive when you sob and weep over the hopelessness of your situation. You learn to work together side by side, as you gather and prepare food, repair clothing, and build a shelter. You laugh together and sigh together, share your dreams, hopes, memories, even your deep-rooted fears. . . .

You can finish the fantasy yourself. Do you think you could fall in love? Do you think you could become man and wife? Do you think maybe you could have a good marriage?

Do you at least think you can now reconsider your criteria?

9

Blind Dates: The Great Adventure

The great epic called marriage often begins with a single step—the blind date.

Alas, much of our life is spent in vicarious living—we live via movies, television, novels, and sporting events. We are voyeurs removed from the action. But there's no vicarious experience on a blind date. To a greater or lesser degree you are the playwright, producer, and director as well as the romantic lead in the drama that unfolds.

The scenario is created by you and your date; it takes place before your eyes as you act and react.

For some reason, however, the blind date has always been something to snicker at, somewhat on a par with mother-in-law jokes. Everyone has a horror story about a blind date of their own or of some friend or relative. Oh, how dreadful or ludicrous the matchup! Oh, the agony and the embarrassment. Imagine, two people wrong for each other condemned to sharing a drink or lunch or even a whole evening!

For many men and women, the blind date is something to be avoided at all costs. "Suppose she doesn't like me?" "Suppose I hate him?" "It's like meeting in a fish bowl." "I'd rather meet someone naturally without all the pressure of a blind date."

Yes, there is risk in a blind date, but there is risk in everything you do. Remember, luck favors the chance taker.

If you never take a chance, you can't win. If you're a sports fan, you know that in every contest the great sports stars are the ones who force the play. They do the unexpected. They take chances and they win.

And what if the date doesn't fulfill the fantasy you've been pursuing, and the date turns out to be just another person like you who's looking and dreaming? Can't you at least be friends? You may have quite a lot in common, despite the apparent mismatch. Why not spend the time sharing a bit of yourselves with each other? Will Rogers once said he never met a man he didn't like. If you share some of his philosophy, you'll never have a wasted blind date. Even if the blind date is doomed to romantic failure, it can still be an enriching human experience. You might even help each other in the great spouse hunt by introducing each other to other friends. Think of a blind date as your lottery ticket to romance!

Speaking for myself, the blind date is one of the few pleasures of being single that I miss. I always thought that the reward of finding that special someone was well worth the risk of a few hours' disappointment. And of the hundreds of happily married couples I interviewed, at least half volunteered that they met through some kind of fix-up or blind date. Almost all of the couples agreed that it was an excellent way for people to find one another. The great majority of women said they too had set up at least one date for a friend or a relative.

I'm reminded of an old story. There was once a man who struggled to support his sick wife and seven children, a difficult and discouraging battle. He was a pious man who prayed to God several times a day. But one day he reached the end of his patience, and he berated God, "Dear God, I've been a good man all these years, and devout too. I prayed every day. I lit candles. I helped my fellow man. I gave to the less fortunate. What would have been so terrible if you had helped me a little? For years I prayed for a little good fortune. And yet I'm still poor. Couldn't you have seen to it that I at least won a lottery?"

There was a great beam of light from the sky and God's voice responded. "Ah, Max, Max," God said, "couldn't you at least buy a ticket?"

In the great lottery of romance, you should at least buy a ticket.

Carol's Story

Let me offer the example of Carol, the wonderful woman who was good enough to marry me some years ago. She had never been married, a truly perplexing condition since she was beautiful, warm, friendly, compassionate, intelligent, successful—and a good dancer!

When I asked her why she had never married, she had the grace and wit to say, "I was waiting for you."

For many years, Carol concentrated on a career in publishing and had considerable success and advancement. One day she realized that she was past thirty, and there was more to life than a career. She told me it was blind dates that kept her spirits up.

"I decided that I could use all the help I could get, and so when anyone mentioned a blind date, I said yes. Why not? I was glad my friends and relatives were thinking of me and were interested in my welfare. Even if they made a mistake, how bad could it be? After all, it was up to me whether I continued to go out with the man again. My attitude was that maybe the next one would be *the* one—and eventually it was.

"I always thanked whoever arranged something and gave them a little report later. You'd be surprised at the number of people who kept me in mind—and kept me socially busy."

Blind dates have another advantage: They give you practice in the art of meeting and getting to know people. An acquaintance of ours was a brilliant scientist in his late thirties. He seemed to be a confirmed bachelor, although everyone agreed he would make a wonderful husband and father. He finally gave in and agreed to go out on a blind date. Over the course of a year, we introduced him to five or six lovely women. He took each of them out, but nothing happened. Then after a silence of several months, he called and told me he was getting married. He thanked me profusely for being such a great matchmaker.

"Which woman was it?" I asked.

"You haven't met her," he replied. "You see, going out on all those blind dates gave me confidence. I used to be uptight with anyone I didn't know. I was so tongue-tied, I guess I appeared irritable or even angry with my dates. After the third or fourth blind date, though, I realized that meeting a new woman wasn't so terrifying. I could handle it. Also, the dates you set up for me helped me crystallize what I wanted in a wife.

"So when I sat next to Helen at a concert, I was able to start a conversation and make a date. We started seeing each other every day, and yesterday we decided to get married."

The Blind Date Equation

You must get past that first date! The overwhelming number of happily married couples didn't fall in love until they had known each other for some time, often for a very long time. Some of them may even admit they really fell in love only after being married a while.

Don't believe all of the people who tell you they fell in love at first sight. Very often they're rewriting history, and they've told the story so often they actually believe it. Check it out with people who knew them when. The love-at-first-sight myth is so strong that many couples fantasize that that's the way it happened.

To give yourself a chance to fall in love you must survive the first meeting. There has to be a second meeting, a second chance, a third meeting and a third chance. The more chances, the greater the odds of winning in the lottery of love.

Here's an interesting way to look at the equation of a blind date. You don't have to be a math whiz to follow this. The most positive reaction is designated "+" and the most negative is "−". A zero is neutral.

First Meeting

	Him	Her		
(a)	+	+	=	+2
(b)	+	0	=	+
(c)	+	−	=	0
(d)	0	+	=	+
(e)	−	+	=	0
(f)	0	0	=	0
(g)	−	−	=	−2

In (a), obviously another date is in order to provide the opportunity to escalate "like" to "love." In (b), he has a positive reaction while she doesn't feel strongly one way or the other. Of course, a second date is called for. He's interested and she may have missed something. In (c), he's interested but she definitely is not. He should try for a second date, and she faces the following dilemma: He really seems to like her and although she wasn't crazy about him, he does have good taste and he did persevere. Why not give it another chance; maybe there's something about him she can learn that will change her mind.

In (d) and (e), you have the same conditions as (b) and (c) but with the genders reversed. You may think this is harder, but it's not. When a woman has a positive reaction and the man is zero, it's like shooting fish in a barrel. What man can resist a woman who likes him? The big hurdle here is that so many women think it's wrong or not ladylike to reveal their true feelings of attraction. Strangely enough, that's what makes a woman almost irresistible to a man. It's the kind of flattery that's impossible to ignore. It makes a man feel good about himself, and he wants more of it. Given a second chance, he may very well decide that the relationship should be encouraged.

So even in the most difficult situation—he's negative and she's positive—a second or third date can dissipate whatever caused the negative reactions in the first place. There's a chance that real romance will blossom. There are thousands of cases where this has happened, perhaps to people you know, who have never told you about it. Check it out!

Even (f) is worth a second date to see if the two neutral feelings can move into the plus column. Thus, in only one of the above equations, (g), do you have a condition in which the relationship may not work. Even here, it may just be the wrong time or the wrong place. Oh, well, there are plenty of good fish in the sea. Let's try another blind date!

My Own Story

One day I was standing in my usual spot on the railroad station platform when Anita, a fellow commuter, hailed me. At that time I'd been a widower for about a year.

"Milton," she said, "I have a lovely girl for you."

"Great," I said, enthusiastically. "What's her name and phone number?"

Anita was pleased with my attitude and I copied all of the information in my little book.

Then I added, "To be fair, I have to tell you I won't be able to take her out for about a year."

"A year? What are you talking about?"

"Every time I get a new name, I put it at the bottom of the list. And recently I decided I shouldn't go out more than two or three times a week. So, as I figure it, it will take about a year to get to her name."

Anita was speechless, so I continued, "But the list moves faster than you'd expect! You know, some of the women meet other people or they move. Some die or make up with their husbands!"

Then Anita demonstrated the savvy that has made her a top literary agent. She said, "I forgot to tell you one thing. Carol is a senior editor at a major publishing house. You could talk to her about your next book."

Lo and behold, Carol's name went straight to the top of the list. And when I got to the office that day, I called her. I was attracted at once by her response because when I introduced myself, she said immediately, "How nice. I've been looking forward to hearing from you." There was none of that embarrassing business of having to explain who I was and why I was calling.

"Can I take you to lunch today?" I asked.

"I'm sorry," she told me, "I have a previous lunch date."

"How about tomorrow, then?"

"Oh, I'm busy then too. What about Friday?"

"Do you realize what you're doing?" I said. "I could be engaged by Friday!"

"That would be very sad," she said.

I suggested we meet at 12:30 on Friday, at the club where I had lunch every day. Full of anticipation, I arrived early and took my regular table. I told the maître d' I was expecting a guest and would order later. But Carol didn't arrive. I looked at my watch—12:40 came and went. So did 12:50. The minutes dragged by. At last, the maître d' showed up with a very attractive lady. The first thing I thought was "Uh-oh. She wears glasses!" (I must say that was the first and last time I ever thought about them.)

The maître d' held the chair out for her, but she didn't sit down. "You must forgive me for being so late," she told me. "I had a last minute call from an out-of-town author, and then the traffic was terrible."

The maître d' was called to another table, leaving us standing together. "Won't you be seated?" I asked.

"First, I have a question for you."

"What's that?" I asked.

"Are you engaged yet?"

When I laughingly replied, "No," she smiled sweetly and said, "Now I'll sit down."

By the end of that memorable meal I knew I had found someone special.

Blind dates. God bless them!

Do's and Don'ts

After much trial and error I arrived at some do's and don'ts about blind dates. There are many well-meaning people who think such dates are awkward and embarrassing, so to take the sting out of it they arrange for a double date. A young married couple trying to match some friends might plan an entire evening for the four of them. Cocktails, dinner, theater, and so on. Now that can be really awkward and embarrassing! What happens is that everyone in the party is under terrific pressure to make it work, so they don't act normally. You not only worry about how you come across to the new person but also about what your friends or relatives think about how you are behaving. Everyone becomes very uptight and unnatural. The ideal way to meet and savor the flavor of someone new is one to one! Yes, it might be awkward at the start. But it's a two-way street, and it's surprising how quickly the unnaturalness fades away. You can cover more ground and make more progress in a half hour, one-on-one, than in five hours with another couple.

An even worse blind date scenario is a first meeting at a large cocktail party or some public function; there are too many distractions. There are too many opportunities for you to hide, to use a buffer, to get lost, or to let your eyes wander. So always plan your first dates for a one-on-one setting, free of environmental distractions or competition. You don't need the additional hurdles. You're there to find out about one another, to act and react to one another, and to show privately the unpublic you. One-on-one, you can reveal what you are like, what you think, what you dream about, what you want.

There's no need, however, to cover all of this at one meeting. A first date is like an appetizer at a long-anticipated banquet. The appetizer should tickle the palate and start the juices flowing. It should be exciting and stimulating, awakening an interest in what is to come. An appetizer and a first date should leave you hungry, looking forward to more, not overstuffed with revelations or intimacies too overwhelming to digest all at once.

Tempt the palate—that's what a first date should do, but what if it does not? If the appetizer is not great or even pretty poor, does that mean you abandon the banquet? No sir, it's the main course you must check out! And while I'm using this metaphor, remember that many a meal is saved by the dessert.

You've been looking for a while but nothing seems to happen. Blind dates, which in anticipation seemed so exciting, turn out to be boring. There's an inclination to be discouraged and a tendency to want to withdraw from the marriage race. Don't do it! Giving up hope is like taking seasonings out of your diet. Without hope, life is tasteless, flat, so much mush.

When I was in elementary school, I read a story that has been an inspiration ever since. There once was a Scottish king, Robert the Bruce (1274–1329), whose country had been invaded by the English. He fought them again and again, and although his armies were brave and true, they were defeated every time. Finally, after one battle there was a complete rout. The king was forced to flee alone and incognito to save his life. He wandered for several days and then found shelter in a peasant's cottage. The farmer didn't recognize him but nevertheless offered him a seat at his hearth and a bowl of porridge. As the king sat there in despair, slowly warming himself, his eye was caught by a spider that was trying to spin a web at the edge of the fireplace. Each time as the web neared completion a gust of air from the chimney tore it down. But the little spider was undaunted; it started over again. After the seventh try, the spider was successful; the web held and was finally completed. The king jumped up, revealed himself to his host, and shouted, "One more time! I shall keep trying one more time until we win!" He gathered together a small band of followers and started a campaign that eventually led to victory for Scotland.

Remember the valiant spider. "One more time!"

Keep trying. The next blind date may be the one to change your life.

10

Enhancing the Catalyst Connection

One of the greatest catalysts for a happy romance is the ability to share playfulness and joy and laughter with each other. As children, we all like to laugh and play. One of the costs of growing up can be the loss of this playfulness. For the sake of being "adult," we smother this basic human yearning for laughter and fun.

Who are the people you like to spend time with? Are they people who are sober and serious, always straining to reach some important public or private goal, always working on some great social problem? The odds are the answer is no. You may respect and admire that kind of dedication, but the people you enjoy spending time with are probably those who take time off for play and laughter with you.

These are the people who work toward even serious goals without taking themselves too seriously and who never forget the human, fun side of life. They are optimistic, cheerful, and confident of their future. They believe everything will turn out all right. They are positive and ready to try new things, explore new ideas and new relationships. Everything about them reflects the fact that they are winners. They are fun to be with; their tempo is upbeat; when you are with them, your spirit dances.

On the other hand, there are people who are always deadly serious, constantly striving and struggling for something, never satisfied. They plod and toil, and they have no time for play. Their view is: "I don't have time for such nonsense. Fooling around is only for children. There is work to be done! If you're going to get somewhere and be somebody, you have to work, not play."

Those who squelch their playful impulses also stunt their capacity to take joy in life. They tend to be a bit withdrawn because they don't like to share their dreams or feelings, and they're not much interested in yours. Actually, they are probably embarrassed when you try to share your feelings with them. They don't have the time or the emotional energy. They're too busy worrying and fretting and sweating out every advance they make. They're afraid of failure and they worry about the future. On the rare occasions when they do share their problems, they bemoan how dreadful life is and what tough breaks they've had.

I'm sure you know people like this. Aren't you glad you're not one of them!

The fact is, that catchy old tune that advises you to accentuate the positive, eliminate the negative, is right on target. If you want to be wanted, you've got to enjoy life and be ready to share your joy. You've got to be unafraid to play, to laugh, to have fun. Remember when you were young: joy and good times were the real world, and your best friend was the person who was the most fun to play with.

Enjoyment is infectious; it resonates in those around you. When you are having a good time, the chances are your companion is too. So when you meet someone for the first time, lighten up. Smile. Have fun. Playfulness entices the catalyst connection. And if your dates don't want to play, it's their bad luck. They're probably not for you!

What's So Funny?

"I don't see what's so funny" can be the death knell for romance. If one of the parties marches to a different drummer about humor, you have a couple that is out of sync. The rat-tat-tat and reverberation of "What's so funny?" will surely destroy the magic rapport that romance needs. The very essence of a happy marriage rests on a compatible sense of humor. This is one of the easiest and earliest tests for foreshadowing your future together. Do you laugh at the same things? Do you have to stop and tell him or her what's so funny? Are you bewildered at his or her convulsions of laughter?

I remember a near mistake I was about to make that was avoided by laughter. After being widowed for a year, I dated an extremely attractive attorney from New York. She seemed to have everything—looks, brains, style, and an interest in marriage. After several dates of escalating interest and promise, I invited her to a dinner dance attended by many of my friends. They were all impressed with her, especially the men, because she was very glamorous. I was having a wonderful time as our table was full of laughter, sparked by one-liners that zipped back and forth around the table like so many Ping-Pong balls. Again and again, she would lean over and whisper in my ear, "What's so funny?" By the end of the evening I knew we were not a couple. She and I were sailing through life on different wavelengths. Life with her would be just so much static.

Creative Listening

Creative listening is a wonderful way to enhance the catalyst connection. Listening is an art and a powerful way of communicating. It's much more than passively hearing what someone is saying. Good listening makes for empathetic understanding and support. It provides instant feedback with the twinkle of an eye, a nod, a small smile of encouragement, a barely audible sound of sympathy. Good listeners let you know they're with you all the way.

Just as women are more open than men about sharing their feelings, they have a greater need to express and share what they feel. Venting to the four walls is not enough; a sympathetic ear is invaluable. But men also need to talk about what's disturbing or perplexing them. A man needs an empathetic ear, as well. When he finds one, he often finds he cannot live without it. What luck for you! You can be that empathetic ear. You can supply the feedback and understanding so vital in human relations.

Revealing Your Emotions

Men generally are much less open than women and do not reveal their emotions easily. They've been brought up to believe that many feelings, like sympathy, sentimentality, nostalgia, even romantic love, are signs of weakness. There are other feelings that are masculine and acceptable, like anger, ambition, passion, loyalty, competition, and gusto.

Men are slow to admit what they feel, even to themselves. This is true even when it comes to love. Nevertheless, men can be helped to discover, recognize, and release their emotions. This provides an important opportunity for a woman. Evoking feelings and enabling a man to recognize and accept his emotions creates a special bonding between the two.

This may sound overwhelming and difficult and involved, but it's not. There is a very easy bridge you can use to reach the new man in your life: *Reveal your own emotions.* Tell him how you feel about things. Share your fears, your affections, your spirit, your fervor. Don't hide your tender heart. Women sometimes attempt to take on the emotional style of men. If he's reticent and withdrawn, she thinks she must be cool and aloof, too, but this is a big mistake. Sharing can be contagious. Bit by bit, he may be encouraged to discuss things with you he never talks about to anyone else. He will discover how much you have in common. He will think of you when you are apart and when he's confronted with something he'd like to bounce off someone. The bond between you will grow. You're on your way to a one-and-only relationship.

People who share their emotions are drawn to each other; a bond is formed between them. Strangers who experience a shared emotion stop being strangers.

Three Tales

Here are three tales that demonstrate the power of sharing an emotion.

Mary, a woman Hugh knew for years, worked in the accounting department and was a pleasant co-worker. She said "Hi" whenever Hugh passed in the hall or elevator; he even enjoyed dancing with her at the office Christmas party. But that was it. They never gave one another a second thought until old "J. P. Moneybags" came by one day and announced that the firm had been sold and everyone was fired with only one week's severance. Hugh hated that man for the boorish arrogant way he did it. He used and discarded all of the employees without a second thought. Hugh was seething. That's when he bumped into Mary in the elevator. She was sobbing. She tried to turn and hide her tears but couldn't help repeating over and over, "That lousy man, that lousy man." Hugh reached out and put his hand on her shoulder to comfort her. After a while she stopped crying, and they shared their anger and despair and contempt as they discussed what had happened.

Then, instead of returning home to their empty apartments, they went out for a drink, which turned into dinner and a movie after they had both thoroughly cussed the rat out. There's a lot of water over the dam now, but it all started with the emotion of despair they shared.

Lois was surprised to see the large turnout at the funeral. Izzy had been a poor old newspaper man, with no family and surely not many friends. How could he have any? He was just a refugee, slowly going blind, who worked at his newsstand seven days a week.

His great talent was his cheerful "Good morning: How are you today?" And he greeted every one of his customers by name. He was a Holocaust survivor who seemed to nurse no bitterness despite the horrors he had experienced at Auschwitz.

Then on Tuesday he was gone. Lois learned that a car with a drunk driver behind the wheel had careened onto the sidewalk and crushed the old man and his little stand. As she thought about his life and death, she was engulfed in sadness and impulsively decided she had to attend his funeral in the little synagogue on the corner. She was determined that his passing should not go unmarked, unnoticed, and ungrieved.

And so as she sat on the hard bench at the service, she was surprised and comforted that others had felt the same way. As she stole a glance around the room, she recognized many of the neighborhood people, each isolated in his own world but sharing a common bond of sympathy for this poor soul who had touched their lives.

When the service was over and Lois was leaving, the man who had been seated next to her said, "What a sad life—and yet somehow inspirational."

"You're right. He certainly brightened his corner," Lois said.

"Say, can I give you a lift somewhere?" the man asked. "I brought my car so that I could get back to work after the service."

They spent only twenty minutes together that day, but the feelings of empathy they shared were the seeds that blossomed into a lifetime love affair.

At first, Bobbie was very grateful when her sister Ann and Ann's fiancé, Fred, said they wanted to take her out for her birthday. She had no plans, and her girlfriends had dates. It was to be a surprise, something "different and exciting." First, there was that long car trip, which added some mystery and glamour. But when they got there—what a letdown! It was a basketball game. Fred was a former basketball player and a complete nut about the game, and Ann had become a fan, too. The team they were rooting for was playing for the divisional championship at their opponents' home court. Bobbie had seen a few high school and college games, and she could easily live without it. It seemed such a waste of energy to her.

When they arrived, the game had already started. Fred was able to find their seats easily among the faithful fans who had followed the team because they were so glum and quiet. Their team was losing and losing badly. By halftime, they were 18 points behind. All around her, Bobbie could hear the groans and catcalls at the outrageously unfair calls made by the referees.

Early in the second half, Bobbie began to get into the game. Even she could see that the visitors were being treated unfairly. She was particularly piqued by the bias of the home team crowd, who yelled and booed when the visitors were shooting. But she learned quickly, and soon she was cheering and screaming whenever their team scored. The team continued to catch up, and when they reached the last forty seconds of play, they were only 4 points behind. The visitors had the ball. They streaked down the field and passed to a man on the outside, who made a miraculous 3-point goal. Now they were only 1 point behind! But the home team had the ball, and all they had to do was stall for fifteen seconds. They played it safe, passed and dribbled to run out the clock. There were only three seconds left when the visitors' "Flash Gordon" stole the ball, took two steps, and let it fly—just as the buzzer ended the game. The ball sailed through the hoop for the winning points! The visiting fans went wild, yelling, screaming, jumping, clapping, and slapping one another.

Fred and Ann were hugging and jumping up and down, and Bobbie was surprised to find that she was doing the same. She was hugging the man who sat next to her, and they were yelling and jumping with the rest. Eventually, they all calmed down, and Bobbie was suddenly terribly embarrassed. She didn't know this man, had hardly said a word to him. How should she act? Should she be annoyed with him? What nerve to grab her like that! But maybe in all of the excitement and euphoria, she had grabbed *him.* Fortunately, when they separated, the man was also embarrassed and very apologetic. When he saw that she accepted his apologies with good humor, he was somewhat emboldened and added, "But you sure are huggable!"

The four of them went out for coffee and a celebration of the victory. The excitement and enthusiasm Bobbie shared with her new friend became the catalyst on which their friendship and marriage was built.

If there is a moral to these stories it is that spontaneous, genuine sharing of emotions can make strangers into friends, and friends who share the same emotions make great partners for life. But if you never let yourself open up, you'll never know.

11

Look Under the Hood

Anyone who drives a car knows that when a car can't be started, sooner or later you have to check under the hood. When you know that you are ready to marry and you have been looking for a while without success, then you too are stalled. You must pop open your hood and take a long thoughtful look at your insides. What's holding you up? What are you doing to prevent yourself from meeting a potential spouse or following up a special relationship? Do you turn others off? Do you turn yourself off? Have you adopted a persona to fit in with all of your single friends who have given up? Do you really want to find someone? Are you afraid?

When you look under the hood to find out what's holding up your happiness, be honest with yourself. The failure to see things as they really are accounts for the inability of many people to achieve happiness. So don't lie; don't pose; don't give yourself the benefit of every close call. You are the mechanic, and it's absolutely confidential; no one else is watching and no one else will hear! Look carefully under your hood for whatever needs repair or adjustment.

Are you, in fact, somewhat selfish, stubborn, self-centered, petulant, crabby, autocratic, willful, a poor loser, or even worse, a bad winner? Could you fall in love with, or even like, someone like yourself? Are you interested in other people, a good listener, kind, helpful, and supportive? Do you like the real you?

Ask as many questions as you need to in order to find the fatal inhibitor. How do I know there is an inhibitor? As a matchmaker for many years, I've learned that anyone who really wants to get married can get married. I've known brides who were too fat or too thin, too short or too tall, too smart or too dumb, ugly, poor, rich, spoiled, nervous, humorless, and boring. I've known grooms who were all of those things too, and bald, short, heavy, uptight, or too macho in addition. Yet every one of those women and men got married and had a chance at happiness.

How about you? Check under your hood. What's holding you up?

At this point, you may say, "What's he talking about? I'm no psychologist. If there is something inhibiting me, if I'm stopping myself, how can I find it alone?"

First, you must believe that you can change. Don't be like the patient my doctor described: "He's enjoying poor health." You're a living, breathing human being, and you have the gift of change. You can make yourself into whatever you want to be. Instead of sticking with whatever you find under the hood, you can become more compassionate, loving, caring, joyful, optimistic, positive, hopeful, and interested in other people: in other words, just the kind of person you want to meet and fall in love with.

Don't think it's impossible; it's not. There are transformations like this going on every day. Don't let embarrassment or pride stand in your way. This is too important. Get started—the new you is only a personal effort away.

You know things about yourself that no one else does. You know on some deep level what is relevant to you and why. You can tap into that level, using whatever abilities you have—reasoning or experience, spiritual tools, or artistic gifts.

Intuition

One invaluable tool that all of us have is intuition. I urge you to use yours to find out what's troubling you. In my book, *Intuition: How to Use It for Success and Happiness* (E.P. Dutton & Co., 1981), I point out:

> The mind's intuitive awareness system is so efficient that it picks up millions of bits of information that completely elude the conscious or logical mind. It stores this information continually, throughout all the years of your life. As a result, you have amassed a vast storehouse of unconscious knowledge, information that you use whether you realize it or not. Indeed, intuition affects much of what you do and what you think.

Your own intuitive system may very well have the answer to what's holding you up. But how do you tap this intuitive storehouse?

One excellent way is to induce a state of meditative relaxation, which often enables you to bridge the gap between your conscious awareness and your intuition. Here is a method that has worked for me and for most of my students:

First, select a place where you'll be alone and free of any noise, music, lights, or the ringing of the telephone. No external distractions.

Sit in a chair or on a couch with your eyes closed, back straight, hands at your sides. As you breathe normally, let all thoughts drop away.

Concentrate on your breathing: shed all other consciousness. Do not try to control the inhaling and exhaling of your breath. Merely observe it. Pay close attention as the air enters your nostrils, moves up through the nasal passages, down into your throat, and fills your lungs.

Note how your chest and stomach expand as the air moves in. And then as the air retraces its path, note how your diaphragm contracts and pushes the air out of your body through nose or mouth. Be aware that something mysterious and wonderful has happened. Your body has taken what it needs from the air and expelled the waste and residue.

Treat the inhale/exhale process as a single cycle that absorbs your total, relaxed attention.

Notice how different parts of your body react as they relax: how uneven your breathing is, and how hard it is to concentrate on your breathing without trying to control it.

To keep your mind from wandering, you may find it easier to concentrate by noticing the number of inhale/exhale cycles completed. Set a goal of fifty or even one hundred cycles.

As you progress through this exercise, you will

become more relaxed and more receptive to subtle feelings, fleeting visions, and odd thoughts that pass through your half-awake mind.

This is a wonderful way to achieve deep relaxation or to fall asleep effortlessly. But to get answers you must ask questions, and the one to ask yourself, in one form or another, should be, "Why am I not married?" Formulate the question in a form you feel comfortable with, such as, "What's holding me up?" or "Am I really ready?" Now present all of the reasons you can think of, and turn each reason over and examine it as closely as you can, using little overt guidance. As images appear, turn them over and look at them, using as little conscious direction as possible. Do not interfere with your body's tendency to cooperate. For example, you will begin to discover perceptible shades of feeling related to each answer, and then gradually (or suddenly) you will begin to feel more strongly about certain "answers."

You will feel more relaxed, more at ease, as you reflect on some matters. You will surprise yourself as you pursue new insights, and new pieces of "evidence" will come to light.

As you continue to use this exercise, you will get better at reaching your intuitive system and at understanding its many messages. You'll soon begin to feel good about the whole process of discovery.

If your mind wanders, simply follow the reverie wherever it leads, asking yourself the magic question: "Why?" Why do you have a vision of your uncle Max, with his big black mustache? The answer may come as an image of his wife Helen, as a bride. Why Helen? The answer may be that you were the flower girl at Max and

Helen's wedding, and Helen, so young and beautiful, died shortly after the marriage. Is this the unconscious reason you've been avoiding marriage all these years?

Intuitive answers come at the strangest times and places. You do not have to be in a state of meditation. However, the problem or question must be asked again and again and repeatedly pondered. No matter how fruitless the search, keep posing the question you are grappling with: Why am I not married? Then, although you may give up thinking about it consciously, your subconscious will still be working on the problem.

This remarkable phenomenon is known as incubation. When you have worked consciously on a problem for a long time with no results, often by breaking off and "sleeping on it," the question answers itself. From out of nowhere the answer pops up at the most unexpected time. It can take a few hours or several months. Although conscious effort is exhausted, your intuitive system still works on it and draws on the millions of bits of information and observations and experiences stored in your mind. When the right combination is hit, the door swings open like a bank vault, and the answer is there.

A twenty-five-year survey done with my classes came up with some of the following answers to the question, "Under what conditions have you found answers to serious problems?"

"While driving in the car alone."
"Sewing late at night."
"Taking a warm slow shower."
"Shucking corn."
"While trying to fall asleep."

"Taking a long walk."
"Just before awakening."
"Listening to classical music."
"Whittling."

There are thousands of answers possible. I mention this phenomenon here to encourage you to be receptive to your answers.

Only you can know; only you can furnish the answer. Only you can recognize that it is in fact an important answer! Learn to trust your intuition and permit it to be your friend and guide.

Friends Can Help

You can't always find answers by yourself. Sometimes talking to a close friend or relative can help, someone whose judgment and integrity you respect and who knows you very well and likes you. It helps to find someone who is supportive, has relatively healthy relationships, and perhaps has been down the same road. Sometimes it is good to talk to a member of the opposite sex. In fact, there are many advantages in talking to the other side. There are perceptions and insights that are singularly male or female, and you may get revelations about how you come across to the other sex that will surprise you.

The wonderful thing about uncovering an unconscious bad habit or emotional hang-up is that very often that's all you need to cure it. Many of our inhibitions melt like morning fog under the light of reason and examination.

Inhibitors fatal to marriage are often based on fear. Here is a partial list of fears that have disturbed other people:

1. Marriage is a trap. I'll suffocate.
2. Nobody can live with me forever.
3. I can't live with someone else forever.
4. I'm not good enough—she (he) will find out.
5. All men are animals.
6. All women are gold diggers.
7. My marriage will turn out like my parents' marriage.
8. I'm too ugly (too fat, too thin, not smart enough, not healthy enough, etc.).
9. My mother (father, sister, brother) needs me.
10. I'll be mortgaging my whole future.
11. It will upset the kids if I remarry.
12. I'll never find another man as a good as Charlie was.
13. I'll lose my alimony.
14. I'll have to give up my career.
15. I'm not ready for children, and what if he (she) wants them now.
16. I can't deal with another divorce.
17. I can't handle sex.

Of all of these fears, sex is often the most deeply rooted. Sexual problems deserve a chapter of their own, which you'll find next.

Are You Being Manipulated?

A not so rare situation occurs when someone wants you

to remain single, for their good rather than yours. Sometimes it's an unconscious wish, manifested in manipulations that wash out all potential candidates.

I'm thinking of the mother who can't bear to let her son go off and marry some strange woman, or the widowed father who thinks of his daughter as the perfect housekeeper for his old age. There are dozens of family situations where the marriage of a son or daughter would upset other family members' plans, and so they create hurdles that are impossible to surmount. No matter who you bring to meet the manipulators, they find some fatal flaw in the potential spouse. It's usually someone who knows you very well, knows your vulnerability, and can manipulate you to do the rejecting yourself. It can even be a close friend who would be all alone if you married. Stop a moment and reflect on whether this situation is part of your experience. A manipulator, or listening to one, may be your fatal inhibitor to marriage.

We have a family story about old "Uncle" Leo who married my mother's cousin Sally many years ago. It seems that Leo was the oldest bachelor in his family. He was twenty-nine at the time he brought Sally home to meet his mother. Sally was twenty-one, beautiful, intelligent, industrious, and in love with Leo.

After the usual tea and cookies, his mother drew him aside and said, "Leo, my dear sweet son, she's very lovely and seems like a nice girl, but there's a problem here—she's too beautiful. Can't you see that she will attract other men? You'll never have a moment's peace; you'll never be sure she's really yours. Find someone you can count on."

She must have sensed that her warning was not

going over as she expected. Leo had become very grim and was breathing deeply. He could barely restrain himself; finally, he hoarsely whispered, "Mama, for the past six years I have brought home eight girls for your approval and blessing. In every case you found something wrong—from 'the wrong family' to 'She laughs like a hyena'—always something is wrong. I am a good son, and I have always heeded your word, but Mama, if you reject Sally—here is my word and my hand—I'll never marry anyone."

Leo and his mother stared intently at each other for several agonizing moments, and then she gave in. "Leo, you silly boy—she has my blessing."

Leo's mama had been forced to see that she had unconsciously wished to keep Leo by her side, and therefore she had rejected all of his potential wives. She was a good mother and could not bear the guilt of having her son go through life unmarried, so she quickly changed her tune.

So when you look under the hood, consider whether or not you are being manipulated by friends or family to avoid marriage. If you are faced with this kind of problem, you must recognize that you have the right to enjoy a full life, and you must also find the strength to take whatever steps are necessary to achieve it.

However, sometimes when you look under the hood you will find a bigger problem than you and your friends can fix. There are wonderful professionals and support groups that can help you identify the part that needs fixing and help you, so don't be afraid to look carefully even if you suspect major repairs may be needed.

12

Sex: The Primal Catalyst

I ronically, sex, the great driving force leading to many marriages—is also a prime cause for unhappiness in many single people.

In our society the preparation for sexual life is woefully inadequate. In other areas of life, shared information is passed on from generation to generation. Knowledge is pooled; the wheat is separated from the chaff; superstitions are dropped and discarded, and what is sound and true survives. Not so with sex. Sex is the big secret, the great miasma stumbled upon by each of us at different times in our journey through childhood. Our readiness for understanding and coping with this powerful force varies enormously, which makes it even harder. Each of us must discover and grapple with sex essentially alone. There's no uniform starting point, no orderly progression, no authoritative coach, no training exercises.

Most tribal societies have rites of passage for sexual indoctrination. However, here in the United States, we're thrown into the great sexual swamp with the hope that we'll learn to swim and survive, doing what comes naturally. For some this powerful force, which sometimes overwhelms our bodies and emotions, creates insurmountable hurdles. Sex education in schools provides a diagrammatic way of looking at sex—like the circulatory system of the body. This may be intellectually understandable, but it doesn't help us cope with the rhythm of our pulse as it surges and throbs with the hormonal changes raging inside us.

Meanwhile, everything around us is colored with sexual hype. From the images on television to the packaging on the supermarket shelves, there is a sexual orientation. We're told subtly that the importance of sex can't be overstated. It permeates every aspect of our lives and perpetuates a perennial state of adolescence.

Little wonder that many of us don't achieve a normal, healthy sex life. This, alas, includes thousands upon thousands of couples who are ostensibly happily married. At least they can have the support and understanding of each other and the potential for sexual accommodation and self-education as a couple.

Sexual Maladjustment

But for singles, sexual maladjustment can be devastating. Singles don't have anyone with whom to share the process of recognizing and changing their hang-ups. Getting some outside help for sexual adjustment is almost always a necessity. So if you suspect that your attitude toward sex is one of your inhibitors to marriage, call in an expert. See a sex therapist, psychologist, or psychiatrist. They can help you achieve some dramatic improvements in this area of your life.

Here are two examples of sexual hang-ups that caused a woman and a man to avoid intimacy and marriage.

Joyce was a pretty child who was pampered by her parents and rewarded for her intelligence and sweet reasonableness. As she approached puberty, her mother began to warn her about boys and how dangerous it was to get involved with them. She told Joyce it was important to remain pure and untouched. Perhaps her mother's warnings came because of Joyce's early physical development. She was the first of all of her peers to develop a full bust and the body that went with maturity. She seemed to be giving off a sexual fragrance that drew boys. Their stares and giggles made her supersensitive to her mother's admonitions. She was always on guard, fighting both the overtures of the young men around her and her own surging emotions.

Kissing and petting were too overwhelming, so she avoided any activities that could lead to them. She loved dancing but would dance only on occasions when it could be kept impersonal. As she made her way through high school and college, there were incidents and evidence that proved her mother was right. All a man ever wanted was sex!

After college, she got on a career track in the art world, where her looks, intelligence, and charm made for rapid advancement. She had some very dear women friends and friendships with homosexual men. Although she dated frequently, no long-term romantic relationships developed. As her friends began to get married, her support circle shrank, and she started to have a sense of foreboding. Her mother's theme now was "Why don't you get married? A girl like you who has everything—what are you waiting for? Picky, picky! You won't be young forever!"

But when Joyce dated someone who might be a potential husband, sooner or later he began to express a physical interest in her. This she would interpret as "He is only interested in one thing!" Then the budding romance would wither. Nothing ever materialized beyond the first few dates.

This sad tale has a happy ending. Joyce had a friend who was the last of the original group to get married. She was a true friend, who continued to see Joyce even after she married and moved away. One day, she and Joyce were having a pleasant lunch together. Joyce was then in her mid-thirties. Her friend said, "Joyce, there's every reason in the world why you should be married. But you're not, and it's not for lack of candidates. I know you're not happy, and my suggestion is to see a therapist—my therapist, to be specific. I started to see him about a year before I got married. I discovered through therapy that I was poisoning all my chances for happiness, and I learned how to overcome my destructive attitudes.

"I'm sure whatever was bugging me is different from what's bugging you. But if you find out what it is, you can cope with it. This therapist is a very sympathetic and perceptive guy. He made all the difference in my life. Why don't you give it a try?"

Joyce followed through, and she discovered that she had a deeply rooted fear of men. However, it could not survive a calm, rational examination of the evidence on which it grew. As this fear was analyzed and put into its proper perspective, Joyce began to enjoy her dates more and some developed into sexual relationships. When they ended, it was for reasons other than sex. She was delighted when she finally met a widower who fulfilled all of her dreams. Now that she's married, she says, when anyone asks her why she waited so long: "I was shackled and handcuffed by my inhibitions and fears."

Luke is a "good ole" Texas boy. He has turned out to be an all-Texas product on the outside but a second-generation Italian on the inside. His family still calls him Luigi. After time spent in college and as a Marine stationed in the Far East, he entered the family construction business. It soon became apparent that he was an excellent man for management; he got along very well with everyone and was universally liked.

He's now in his mid-forties, financially successful, very dependable, highly thought of by the community, and a favorite uncle of a dozen nieces and nephews. But he has never married. He's not homosexual; he enjoys the company of women and likes them. But he has never established a relationship with any woman.

Not long ago, one of Luke's oldest friends had a serious talk with him about his marital status. Luke said, "Sure, I'd like to get married. Maybe I'll have to go back to Italy to find a bride, just like my father did."

"There are dozens of great women right here who'd go for you like a shot," his friend said. "Luke, we've known each other for years and I know everything about you: who you like, where it hurts, how much money you've got, and so on. But you've never mentioned making it with anyone. Every time I bring up the subject, you switch it. Now I'm asking point-blank: Have you ever had sex?"

"OK, old buddy, it's a good thing I know you're asking this for my own good," Luke responded. "I had a couple of lousy experiences when I was real young, and that's put the kibosh on sex ever since." Luke told his friend the following story.

When Luke was just seventeen, he took a pretty young girl named Susanna to the junior prom. He had had a crush on her for years but had never worked up the courage to talk to her before their prom date. It started out as a wonderful evening. She looked gorgeous and sexy in her formal gown. They were dancing to a slow dreamy number when she dropped her head on his shoulder and snuggled up to him closer than before. Her perfume, the warmth of her body, and the sheer deliciousness of the situation were too much for Luke. When he felt her undulating body press closer to his, he was overwhelmed and experienced an erection and an ejaculation. Nobody, including Susanna, was aware of it, but Luke thought everyone in the room must know. It was the worst moment in his life, and he never really recovered from it.

From then on he avoided any activity that could result in a repeat of that nightmare. He avoided close contact with women, even to the point of not sitting next to an attractive woman in a car or on a couch. On the rare occasions when he dated, it was always in a group. He maintained the front of being an interested, eligible bachelor, but he avoided all intimacy.

Unlike Joyce's story, Luke's doesn't have a happy ending. Despite the urging of his best friend, he has absolutely rejected the idea of seeking professional help. He is probably doomed to a life of lonely, celibate bachelorhood.

If you suspect that sex may be an inhibitor for you, don't take chances—get expert help. Don't sit around and wait for things to straighten out. You'll miss the whole parade.

Sexual Choices

Sex can be a Pandora's box. The questions it raises, the stresses and anxieties it creates are inflamed by the needs and drives of the individual and the needs and morals of society. It's all exacerbated by the revolutionary changes in attitudes toward sex. Today's sexual freedom gives rise to new problems singles never had to face before. Aside from the real dangers of sexually transmitted diseases such as AIDS, syphilis, herpes, and gonorrhea, it's an individual's problem to decide how much casual sex to have, with whom, and under what circumstances and how much importance should be ascribed to it. All of these issues require decisions that must be addressed by you and you alone. I would not presume to suggest to you standards for what is right and wrong.

I have avoided taking a stand on whether you should have premarital sex or abstain until after you're married. This is too important a decision to be made by anyone but the individuals involved. There are vital considerations to be weighed on either side of the question.

On the one hand, the case for abstinence is deeply

rooted in our religious and traditional cultures, our family mores and morals. Abstinence is also safer, leaving you unexposed to the dangers of sexually transmitted diseases or pregnancy. It frees you from guilt and the burden of secrecy. It puts off the anxiety of how you'll perform until such time as there is a mutual commitment to each other, ensuring that you'll be together until it does work. It also ensures that the sexual drive will still be there until after the ceremony.

On the other hand, the case for prenuptial sex is based on the recognition that sex in a marriage is very important, and therefore some sampling should be done to see whether in fact you are compatible. The sex drive in people of marriageable age is very great. If you don't share it in basically the same way, there is the strong possibility that one of you could seek it elsewhere, opening up the specter of disease and infidelity.

Another aspect is that you're so much in love, it's only a question of time and convenience before you marry, so why wait and torture youself? It relieves sexual tension during the long wait.

There is also the argument that premarital sex takes the overwhelming importance out of sex. It neutralizes it and enables the people involved to look at marriage in its larger context. Alas, too many marriages fail because they shared nothing but sex.

I'm sure there are other reasons for one approach or the other, and I'll not belabor them all. This is a decision you must make for yourself. But I do think it is very important for you to put sex in its proper place.

Yes, sex is important—it's basic; and a marriage without sex is destined for unhappiness. But does marriage have to provide the best sex you've ever had?

Hardly! If that were the case, you'd have to keep testing to see if there was better sex available with the next date—not the greatest prescription for a happy and satisfying marriage.

Marriage in your life must be something more important than sex, more than mere physical gratification. Marriage is a process of acquiring and developing a best friend who loves and cares for you. Someone you want to be a parent of your children. Someone you can trust and count on. Someone you want to spend your whole life with, yes, in sickness and in health.

If you're concerned with the problem of giving up sex with all others for the balance of your life when you marry, weigh that against the alternative: spending the rest of your life alone. Do you want to be constantly looking for new partners, new one-night stands, where the only interest they have in you is that reciprocal physical gratification, which they measure against what they've had before? It's a sorry substitute for home and family.

Sex is very much like food. You need it to nourish life. But bread and cheese do just fine. You can live without caviar and champagne every night of your life.

One of the great advantages of marriage is that it creates and encourages intimacy, the kind of opening up to each other that may never be achieved in any other relationship. If there are hang-ups or problems with sex, physical or psychological, there is the great advantage of being able to work them out with your spouse, free of the fear of rejection or ridicule that best friends need not fear.

The nicest part about sex in marriage is that it is

happily sanctioned. It has everyone's blessing. You can pick the perfect time and place to share your sexual desires. You need no excuses or white lies to cover your tracks. You don't have to prove yourself; you're married—you have a total commitment to each other. Your partner is not going to steal out in the morning, never to be heard from again!

Marriage has been around a long time, and good wholesome sex has always been a part of it.

13

The Chameleon Effect

D o people see the real you? Or do they see only the persona that you allow them to see? The chameleon is a small lizard that has the ability to change its color and outward appearance, allowing it to blend into its environment and escape detection. Some of us, too, use protective coloring to blend in with our environment, adopting postures and masks to hide our real selves. This is a survival tool for lizards, but in humans, the chameleon effect can be reflective of a poor self-image and a low sense of worth.

Sometimes we try to create an image that we think will improve our chances for success, happiness, or protection. But the chameleon effect is deadly in the great quest to find a mate. If there was ever a need for honesty and openness, it is greatest when you are dealing with a potential spouse.

Intimacy creates the foundation for deep friendships. There is a great hunger in each of us to have intimate friends and that most special friend, a spouse. How wonderful to have someone you can trust completely with your true self. Intimacy is achieved when you are open to another and your true self is revealed. In real friendships, the openness is reciprocal, and you share each other's fears, foibles, dreams, aspirations, and innermost thoughts.

Sex is only a small part of an intimate relationship, though the phrase "having intimate relations" has come to mean "having sex." You can have sex without intimacy, and friends can achieve intimacy without sex. One of the great blessings of marriage is the potential to have both. With intimacy comes vulnerability, susceptibility to hurt, and unprotectedness. It is the ultimate level of trust, and it is therefore rare and special.

Who Are You Kidding?

When you put on an act and pretend to be what you are not, who are you kidding? Who are you trying to fool? If you meet someone who is a potential spouse, and you adopt a persona that is actually successful in fooling that someone, what have you accomplished? You may end up with a marriage in which you'll always have to wear that mask, where you'll never be able to be yourself. How horrible!

One of the great blessings of having a husband or wife is that you have someone who loves you, warts and all. Perhaps at the beginning you decided that the only way you could attract or hold someone was to assume a certain pose, and it worked. He's attracted, and you keep posing. But what if he really fell in love with the mask and not with you?

As soon as you can, in the discovery phase of your

friendship, drop the mask, drop the act, be yourself, and see how it goes. If this results in total disillusionment and the breakup of the budding romance, so be it. Count yourself lucky that it happened early. Who wants to live a double life!

Dropping the mask can have immediate rewards. Take the case of Joan, who was a very dear friend of my cousin Lola. As single career women, Joan and Lola would go to parties together, double date, and share long vacations. They were a perfect team, both in their early thirties, both intelligent, attractive, and good company. They were alike in their desire to find a suitable husband but very different in their personalities and style. My cousin was dark, very sweet, feminine, and empathetic. Joan was blond, sophisticated, skilled in repartee, and fond of one-liners. She was popular with many men who were attracted by her open give-and-take conversation and accepted her as one of the boys. She had many dates but no proposals she could seriously consider.

After Lola was married, she set up many occasions when Joan would join Lola and her husband. But after each visit, she'd be filled with sadness. She felt that somehow she had abandoned Joan. For years, they had shared their dreams and spent so much time pursuing their common goals. Now Lola had achieved her goal of marriage and was very happy. She wanted to help her friend find happiness, and she shared her feelings with me. "Use some of your matchmaking magic for Joan," Lola urged me. "You know, deep down she is a very shy, sensitive girl despite the big front she puts on."

"Lola," I said. "Don't you realize that Joan doesn't need any help attracting men or getting dates? She's terrific at that. Her problem is that she's sending the wrong message. She gives everyone the impression that she's a big swinger, a great party girl. She scares off wholesome guys who are interested in settling down. She's got to give people a chance to see her as she really is."

At Lola's insistence, I talked to Joan at the next opportunity and told her what I thought. Our chat lasted over two hours, and I learned that what Lola had said was true: Joan was essentially shy and sensitive and even timid under that "tough" exterior.

As we were parting, I said, "Joan, you've got to change your act. Why don't you give the men a chance to find the wholesomeness you've been hiding all these years?"

Three days later I got a lovely note from Joan thanking me for my interest and advice. More important, she wrote that she was going to make some changes.

Within a year, I got the joyful news that Joan was engaged. All that was needed was for Joan to drop the mask she had been hiding behind.

Now let's look at this from the other side: a man in your life has adopted a pose and you love it. He projects himself as strong and independent, a man who is captain of his own destiny, who loves adventure and plays for high stakes in the game of life. He builds on this image as your relationship grows. You are especially attracted because there's never been anyone as strong in your life. You fail to see beyond the charade, and you marry, trusting that you have finally found the man you want. Sooner or later the mask will be removed, probably in a time of crisis, and you will be left with an ordinary man, who needs to make himself appear bigger than he actually is. Your disappointment could wipe out your feeling for him, in spite of the fact that if you had known him as he really was in the beginning, all strengths and weaknesses revealed, you might have loved him anyway. And you would have been better prepared for the times when he couldn't be your superhero.

When to Show Your True Colors

What if the chameleon is you? You've met someone, and the relationship is escalating toward love and marriage. Should you tell him that you really didn't go to a private school when you lived in New Orleans, that your father didn't own a large manufacturing plant, and that your mother didn't die when you were twelve?

By all means, yes. Get it out and on the table while you still control the time and place for owning up. No one can present your case better than you. If he or she can't understand and condone your indiscretion then that person is not right for you. Do it early—it is easier, and not much is lost if the relationship falters. On the other hand, it's much harder to be forgiven if you confess after you have made long-term plans to be together.

The commonness of chameleon behavior in dating should make you realize that your date has probably been misled by others before you. He or she will certainly appreciate your honesty in contrast to the other storytellers who have preceded you. Give yourselves ample time in your courtship to let the truth unfold prior to walking down the aisle. Lies and omissions between married partners are much more serious offenses and a lot harder to amend.

Packaging is very important. It catches the eye, creates the impulse, and gets things started. But for real satisfaction it's the product that counts, not the trappings. For a lasting relationship, don't try to fool one another.

Let me tell you a story of a man who, in revealing himself, quite by accident, won the woman of his dreams.

Judy was turned off by Jake's macho affectations. Among other things, he wore his shirt open two or three buttons down so that you could see the curly black hair on his chest as well as several gold chains. But he seemed to be smitten with Judy and kept trying to make a date. One Saturday he called and asked if she'd like to go to the movies. Normally, Judy would have been insulted by the last-minute request and would have turned him down. But there was a movie she really wanted to see, so she accepted, more for the movie than the company. The film was Woody Allen's *Interiors*, a touching and sensitive drama about family relations. Halfway through the film, Judy sensed some movement beside her and noticed Mr. Macho surreptitiously wiping away a tear in the dark.

"I saw him in a new perspective," Judy told me years after the event. "I saw that there was a real human being beneath the facade."

The tear changed everything. It gave her a chance to learn about and appreciate many of Jake's sensitive and good qualities. The interaction that followed changed both of them for the better. Judy and Jake have now been happily married for six years. He leaves only one button open on his shirt—and she wears the gold chains.

Coping with a Chameleon

How do you cope with the chameleon effect? When you meet someone new and you are attracted, there is a very exciting period when you're finding out about each other. Little things start to indicate that this is someone you could like, maybe even love. There is a great tendency to fill in all the spaces with answers you want to hear, whether they are true or not. You start out by accepting each other at face value. It never occurs to you that this is a false front; you want to believe.

When you find yourself in this position with someone you regard as a finalist, I recommend exposure to your friends and family, particularly at family functions—sharing activities with your old friends and meeting his or her friends and family in the same way.

It is a very fine actor indeed who can maintain a false front without giving away clues that you should be able to pick up. Somewhere along the way he or she will reveal an inconsistency, an exaggeration, a deviation from the story you've accepted and embraced. Does that mean it's the end—it's all over? Not at all. All of us tell little white lies; we all exaggerate a little. It's really a question of degree. I had a friend who would say, "I can live with that" when he was faced with any upsetting news. You must be able to say "I can live with that" in a spouse. What must be done is an honest, open appraisal. You must look at him or her with open eyes. That's what parents are for. The total, impartial examination by your father or mother, who hopefully is not bewitched, as you are, may uncover the man or woman behind the mask. (That's how all of the mother-in-law jokes got started! The potential spouse is exposed to the critical future mother-in-law during this examination period.)

Seriously, however, it doesn't have to be your mother or dad; any one of your friends or family will do. They may size up your potential spouse with different eyes. Listen to them, but don't allow yourself to be swept away. Be a bit skeptical about their opinions. Is there a conflict of interest?

Set it all on your balancing scale and make your own decision.

I remember an incident in my youth that identified a chameleon by the process I've described.

In my senior year at college, I met a very beautiful girl whom I'll call Kay. She was a sophomore. In those days, we commuted from home to school. We shared the trip to and from school every day, and in a short time we became close. She was very attractive, with jet black hair adorned by a dramatic widow's peak atop her creamy white face, very dark eyes, and a ruby rosebud mouth. I was enraptured and couldn't wait until the family met her. Finally, I was able to introduce her to my sister, who chatted with her for about an hour in the park one day.

Later that evening, wearing a rather self-satisfied smile, I asked my sister what she thought of Kay. I was incensed when she flippantly said, "Oh, boy, is she a phony!"

"Oh, yeah, you're just jealous because she's so gorgeous."

"How gorgeous can she be under all that makeup? And how about that widow's peak she shaves into place?"

The next day I made a special effort to look at her very closely. I found that the "widow's peak" was indeed shaved and then penciled in.

But that did not squelch my ardor. I could live with that. I knew all the girls used makeup. She was still gorgeous, and my sister was jealous.

About a week later Kay invited me home to listen to some of her records. I was greeted at the door by her father, a quiet middle-aged man who excused himself early and went off to bed after we were seated in the living room. Her mother was a gentle, round-faced woman who was anxious to make me feel at home, serving me fruit and soda. Kay left the room for a while, and her mother filled me in on the wonders of her remarkable daughter. She was so good, so smart, so talented—she could sew, cook, and manage a household. I listened intently; it was all music to my ears. She was not only beautiful, she would make a perfect wife.

Toward the end of these remarks, Kay returned to the room with a piece of cloth she was embroidering. I was truly impressed to see her quietly stitching away as I chatted with her mother. A touching scene. Then I noticed that her mother was becoming increasingly agitated. She began talking faster and faster, and her eyes kept coming back to her daughter's stitching. Finally, I looked too. Kay was unconsciously sewing the cloth onto her dress. Her mother abruptly left the room and after a moment or two called to her daughter. Kay left the room, embroidery and all. When she returned, I could see where the cloth had been cut away.

When I left that evening, I sadly concluded that my sister was right. She might be a phony. In the days that followed, I found more and more evidence that Kay was not the girl I thought, and we drifted apart. I often wondered whether I would have fallen in love with the real Kay if I had met her first. The deception spoiled everything.

14

The Art of Wooing

T he dictionary defines wooing as seeking someone's affections with the intent to marry. There
was a time when everyone accepted wooing as
one of the stages of romance. Today most single people
think there is something terribly old-fashioned about
wooing anyone for marriage. Nonsense. If I had a building block for every marriage that resulted from the
efforts of wooing, I could build a cathedral.

Wooing achieves two very important results. First,
it gives the wooer a chance to deliver his or her message.
What can be more persuasive than a series of actions
and symbolic gestures that say: "I love you, I want you,
I think you're special." It's powerful medicine. Wooers
must be very serious about their intentions or they
would never risk the rejection. That's what makes wooing so effective with the woo-ee. Who can resist its
strong appeal?

Less obvious and just as important, wooing re-
moves the doubt about how the other person feels.
When you know that someone really likes you, you can

relax and allow yourself to think, "He's not so bad," or "I should give her a chance."

Wooing calls for considerable courage; it requires you to expose your feelings and to risk being rejected or made to feel foolish. But if you think you've found someone who could be your best friend and lover, don't you think an all-out effort is warranted? If you put in only one-tenth of the time, effort, and ingenuity you use to make your business or career a success, your chances for romantic happiness would zoom.

Maybe you think it's fine if someone woos you but totally reject the notion that *you* might woo someone you care about. "If he's not willing to run after me, why should I run after him?" The traditional view was that the man did all of the wooing, and the woman was the one wooed. But if you dig a little deeper, you'll find that wooing has always been an equal opportunity activity. Check with your parents and grandparents; you may be surprised to learn how much wooing occurred, and who was the real wooer.

So don't wait for lightning to strike you—get charged up and do your own sparking.

The Catalyst of Wooing

Murray is a short, graying, hardworking man who has achieved considerable success over the years. He's happily married and the father of three children. When questioned about the catalyst that led to his marriage, he said, "I was a confirmed bachelor in my forties. I had had many girlfriends, and I guess some would have liked to marry me. But I was busy with my business, and finding sex wasn't a problem, so I thought: Who needs marriage? Then one day Rose came along. She was attractive and fun to be with, but so were most of the others. The difference was that she was persistent. I'll explain what I mean.

"After we had known each other for a short time, she let me know that she liked me and was very attentive in many ways. After I had taken her to dinner a few times, she cooked dinner for me. She bought me a tie or other little gifts a few times and arranged a surprise dinner party for my birthday. She sent me a valentine, picked me up when I had to work overtime, and bought a shawl for my mother after they met.

"I was flattered, of course, but I sort of laughed it off. But she kept working on it. I told her I was a confirmed bachelor and too old for her. She paid no attention. She was very sweet and kept telling me how much she loved me. Finally I asked myself what I was running away from. Maybe marriage could be good. So I did it.

"Yes, I'm happy. It was the best move I ever made in my whole life. If she hadn't been so persistent, though, it would never have happened. Have you met my children yet?"

Rose told me her side of the story. "Murray wasn't really interested in marriage," she said. "I tried to show him how I felt and how it would be if we married. There were times when maybe I overdid it. But since I always felt good doing things for him, I continued. Then one day I said, 'Murray, why don't we get married?' And he said, 'Why not?'"

Rose had been married once before when she was

very young, just to get away from an unhappy home. Her parents were always fighting, and there wasn't enough money. Her first marriage was an unhappy one. Her teenage idol husband turned out to be an egocentric, spoiled brat, and the marriage lasted less than a year. Then followed many years of unsatisfying relationships and loneliness. Finally Rose met Murray. As the relationship developed, she had some reservations. He was short and plump with gray sideburns. But one day she realized that this was it. "He was so steady and predictable and innately good. Even when he was lying, it was predictable and understandable. He was a haven of security and serenity. How could I help loving him? We've been married over twenty years, and we have three wonderful children and a home in Scarsdale. It is a marriage that was meant to be—but I sure helped!"

For Diana, the catalyst of wooing changed a friendship into a romance. Diana is an intelligent blonde with lively, searching eyes. She is the top buyer of housewares for a large department store, an obviously successful career woman, now in her mid-thirties. She has been married a little over a year. She told me, "As to your catalyst question, there was no one single incident, but maybe this is what you mean. I'd known Martin for several years. We lived in the same apartment house, often met in the laundry room, bumped into each other in the elevator, that sort of thing. He'd help me with packages; I'd buy a paper for him. He had the keys to my car, and I had his in case there was an emergency. I certainly didn't think of Martin as a potential husband. He was a little younger than I, kind of short, and, I thought, not very ambitious. I always intended to marry someone who was smarter and more successful than I was.

"However, we became pretty good friends and even had dinner occasionally. I treated him as a confidant, a kind of best buddy. I'd discuss my dates with him and get his advice on how to handle them. I knew he liked me, but that was all. There was no chemistry.

"Then one night as I was trying to fall asleep—it was a peaceful, snowy evening in winter—I began to think about Martin. I remembered the first time we had dinner together. We were eating at a Chinese restaurant; we couldn't finish all the delicious dishes he ordered, and he had them wrapped to take home. When we got to his car, I was surprised to see he had a picnic cooler in it. (It was summertime and very hot.) Then he suggested a movie, and after we got home, he insisted I take all the delicious food. Kind of sweet.

"Then there was the morning when there were a lot of cars in the railroad commuter lot, and I had to park my car far down at the end. When I got home late from the city, the parking lot was dark and there were very few people around. I hurried to where I'd parked my car but was shocked to find it gone. I went back to the station to call the police, when suddenly I saw my car, parked in the number one spot. I rushed over and found a teddy bear behind the wheel with a note pinned to him that read: 'Diana, you deserve the best spot.' It was from Martin, of course. Every time after that when I got home late from the city, my car would be moved and waiting for me up front.

"Then I thought about the time I went to a big singles dance in New Jersey. My girlfriend had raved about it because it was planned so that there would be more men than women. There *were* plenty of men, but evidently not the right ones for me. Maybe I was too serious, I don't know, but I just didn't connect. The crowd started to thin out and couple up. My girlfriend was one of the people who left with someone. I didn't begrudge her, but I was feeling kind of blue, when suddenly I saw Martin walking toward me.

" 'Where did you come from?' I asked him.

" 'I've been around,' Martin said. 'It's just that you never see me. I was told there'd be some special women here, and there are! May I have this dance?'

"As I lay in my nice warm bed, it came to me: Martin was always there for me. I realized that he was not so short and that he was ambitious in his own way. He is gentle, loving, and very dear. In the year we've been married, there's all the chemistry I can handle!"

How to Target Your Wooing

Wooing works for both men and women; you will be amazed to find how effective it is. But before you play with this magic, you should be pretty sure you really want the person you plan to woo. Here's an exercise that will help you pick the right man or woman.

Earlier I said there are probably hundreds, maybe thousands of potential spouses for you to marry. Waiting for the perfect one to show up is like waiting at the train station for your plane to land. At some point you must declare: "I want to get married, and I'm prepared to make the changes and do the wooing it takes to get results.

"But which one of all the men (or women) I know is best for me?" (They do not necessarily have to be those you've gone out with or even know socially yet.) Here is a chart (Figure 1) that will be a handy tool to help you. This one was developed from a woman's point of view, but can easily be adapted for men.

Set up a chart similar to Figure 1. List all of the single men you know that qualify as potential husbands. In the appropriate column, identify the criteria you now think important in a husband. The more specific and detailed the criteria you list, the more effective this evaluation.

This exercise must be done with the utmost honesty. If you don't play it straight, you'll only be hurting yourself.

Now, evaluate the criteria for each candidate: 1 for the lowest, 2 for average or acceptable, and 3 for most superior.

For example, Harry is just about average height and a bit plump but has wonderful eyes. He's a manager of a local supermarket, goes to the same church as you, has never been married, never been to college, has an open, friendly personality, and a good sense of humor.

Peter is very handsome, was born in Italy, also goes to your church, graduated from the University of Palermo, and is the M.D. for your union; very sophisticated, divorced, seems to be a bit of a playboy.

John is in the advertising business—lots of fun, no religious affiliation, Ivy League graduate, very sensitive and honest, getting very bald but looks good in a suit.

Howard is very rich, comes from a prominent family, does not seem to be religious. He's charming but very reserved and backs away from any physical contact.

Evaluation Chart

Potential Husbands	Physical Attraction	Status	Economics	Religion	Education	Loving and Caring	Honorable

Figure 1

He attended a small local college, acts very proper and correct, is a widower.

Phillip is the shortest of the group, but very sexy. He's ambitious, working on an M.B.A. at night. He's an atheist, very loving, and fun to be with.

Geoffrey is your fantasy lover, your childhood dream of Prince Charming on a white horse. Being perfect, he lives in a never-never land.

Fill in each box in Figure 2 as you judge each candidate for physical attraction. Harry would get a 2; Peter, a 3; John, a 2; Howard, a 2; Phillip, a 2+. After all the boxes are filled, it will be easier to decide who is best for you. Note that Geoffrey, your fantasy lover, is based on the male lead in a soap opera. In real life he has been married and divorced several times, has abandoned his children, and was recently arrested for drug abuse.

Of course, some criteria are more important than others, and that should be factored in. If religion is extremely important, only the first two men would make the cut, and it would be easy to choose between them. If money was your overwhelming consideration, then Howard would probably be your choice.

In any event, the chart and how you fill it out is uniquely yours. Nobody can do it for you and nobody should. If you do a thorough job, you will pick a man worth wooing.

Although these charts are designed for a woman evaluating potential husbands, they work just as well for men looking for a wife. It's ironic that most women think the chart is more valuable for men—because men have more to say in choosing a wife than women do in choosing a husband. This notion is far from the truth.

Evaluation Chart

Potential Husbands	Physical Attraction	Status	Economics	Religion	Education	Loving and Caring	Honorable
Harry (Your Grocer)	2	1	2	3	1	3	3
Peter (Your Doctor)	3	3	2	3	3	1	1
John (Your Neighbor)	2	2	2	1	3	3	2
Howard (Your Landlord)	2	3	3	1	2	2	2
Phillip (Your Co-worker)	2	2	2	1	3	3	2
Geoffrey (Your Fantasy Lover)	3	3	3	3	3	3	3

Figure 2

At this very moment I can think of a half dozen men I know avidly looking for a wife for over a year, ranging from an M.B.A. in his twenties to a very successful lawyer in his early sixties. All of these men will make great husbands, but first they must make some changes and undertake the art of wooing the object of their affections.

No one questions the propriety of a business soliciting a customer or a salesman pursuing a potential buyer. Why be timid about going after the most important contract in your life—the marriage contract?

How to Market Yourself

Wooing is an art, and it poses all of the problems an artist faces. What color for the background? Where is the center of attention? Should the message be symbolic or literal, and so on. All of the do's and don'ts of wooing must be determined and influenced by who you are and who he or she is. What and when you do something is determined by the reactions you get. The wooer can learn from the advertising fraternity.

What is an advertiser's objective? To persuade and motivate someone to choose his product or service. First he must get your attention, and then he must demonstrate that it will be good for you to buy or use what he's selling. This is done through an advertising campaign. A series of commercials (radio, TV, or print) is unfolded, each designed to highlight some important feature. And each commercial is repeated again and again until there is no doubt that the message has been driven home. Some features are more important than others, and more commercial time and effort are spent on them.

For example:

1. The product is healthy.
2. It's tasty.
3. It's free of salt or sugar.
4. It has no fat, no cholesterol.
5. It will give you energy.
6. It's very easy to use.

Then some market research is done. Each of the product's features is tested by running commercials in different comparable markets. The results are carefully noted. Then the most effective feature is highlighted in a series of commercials until the market is won.

When you're wooing someone, it's a lot easier— you've already identified the market. All you have to do is persuade and motivate. Think of all the ways in which you can get this started.

1. Great personal attention.
2. Invitations for theater, movies, etc.
3. Gifts and flowers, books, novelties, perfumes.
4. Helping with a chore like moving or washing the car.
5. Going for a meal together.
6. Introducing your friends.
7. Sharing your thoughts and dreams.

Pick out the best ones and start your campaign. Wooing is never a single commercial. It's a series of concrete acts over a period of time that demonstrates how you feel. Wooing makes it almost impossible for him or her not to realize that you're sincere, very loving, and prepared to make a lifetime commitment.

Proper wooing makes it so easy for the targeted one to finally say, "Why not?"

Sometimes the wooing is not something you give or do but rather how you change—how you change yourself! Here I'm reminded of the wonderful world of the birds and bees and especially the flowers.

Have you ever wondered about the fantastic number of different flowers there are—the profusion of color, size, shape, fragrance, and even where they originally came from? All of this has come about through the need to adapt and change in order to survive. The flower must attract bees and insects, and the surviving species must change and develop new colors, shapes, fragrance, and nectar that will appeal, or it's out of the race for procreation and survival.

What has that to do with you? Sometimes the most important kind of wooing requires changes in yourself. If the object of your affection is turned off by your drinking or smoking or overeating, the most eloquent wooing you can do is to make changes in yourself that will remove the hurdle. This is not easy, but it's very persuasive, and it's probably good for you, too. It's an eloquent demonstration of how much you care and to what lengths you will go to find favor. It's much more than a material gift; it's a positive reaction to his or her preferences. Such a powerful example of flexibility and compatibility will make the object of your affection look a lot closer at your "3's" when he puts you into his wooing chart.

15

The Joy of Nurturing

Wooing never really stops; it just evolves into the next step, which is nurturing. After the initial sexual and emotional attraction, marriage needs more than excitement to keep love alive. In a happy marriage, ongoing, reciprocal nurturing sustains the relationship. This is what makes for true and enduring love.

Falling in love right away is as rare as planting a seed, watering it, and expecting it to burst into full bloom the same day. The miracle in the seed needs nurturing, a healthy environment, and time to germinate. We all need nurturing. It makes us feel loved and important. It creates a sense of self-worth. This strengthening of ego enables us to perform reciprocal nurturing of our spouses. The loving relationship of the "one and only" comes with nurturing within the environment of marriage.

When we first think about nurturing, we imagine nurturing infants and children. But nurturing is also the art of supporting development and growth in adults—family, friends, and loved ones. It is one of the wonderful qualities often ascribed to women. Less recognized, however, is that it is also a masculine trait. In fact, the willingness and ability to nurture—for both men and women—is what turns people from individuals into families. Nurturing is the unselfish extension of help from one human being to another. It is any action that promotes development and growth, comfort or peace of soul; it feeds and nourishes, it educates and trains, it helps us cope with life's roller coaster rides.

As we mature, we begin to understand more deeply our need for nurturing. It blesses both the giver and receiver. Reaching out to help someone endears you to others, whether it's your child, your husband, your wife, your parent, your friend, or your neighbor. The receiver's gratitude may be unexpressed and undemonstrated, but it is nevertheless an important foundation for love.

Nurturing doesn't rate very high with young people. Adolescents and young singles are still influenced by their dream of a perfect love, the great romance of the fairy tale, where love is all wrapped up in that ethereal kiss that lasts eternally: They lived happily ever after. But what happens after the happy ending?

The immature are rarely aware of any need for nurturing. Many are still being nurtured by their parents and think it should always be that way. They expect it as their due. They are very slow to awaken to the responsibility of nurturing others. On the other hand, there are some young people who do understand the importance of nurturing, and they factor it into their choice of partners.

Some people realize fairly early in life that there are times when they must help, when they must pick up the ball and run with it, when they must do the dirty job, when they must support and even carry their friends or family.

In every thoughtful list of what we'd like in a mate, man or woman, there should be the quality of generosity, which is the willingness to give or share, to be unselfish, free of pettiness or meanness. Generosity is the rock foundation of a happy marriage, and nurturing is the most personal way of demonstrating this quality of generosity. Extending yourself to help, anticipating the need for help and concerning yourself with another's problems or pain are all touching forms of wooing.

Nurturing Can Change Lives

Sybil's story speaks quite eloquently on this subject. When she was in high school, an accidental blow to her head left Sybil with one eye pulled off center, and looking up and out toward her ear. She was quite beautiful and intelligent, but this defect caused her such embarrassment and pain that she withdrew from her friends and school. Ultimately, she found a low-paying job. For years, she led a rather lonely, sad life until she met Matt. He worked in the same building. They met in the elevator. He smiled at her, always said good morning, and was very pleasant and cheerful.

Nevertheless Sybil dreaded meeting him every day, not because of how she felt she looked but rather because of *his* appearance. He was spastic. There was rarely a minute that went by without his body twitching;

his mouth twisted when he talked, and he had great difficulty controlling his saliva. It took the greatest control on his part to talk and look at someone at the same time.

When Matt spoke to her, Sybil felt it attracted everyone else's attention to her and her eyes. But then one day she realized that when he spoke to her, he drew more attention to himself than to her. After a while she began to think he was rather heroic in the way he faced the world, and in time they became friends. They shared lunch, long walks, long talks, and personal confidences. Surprisingly, it turned out that Matt had put himself through college and was now an accountant, rather successful despite his handicap. He was particularly effective on tax audits and court appearances.

When they exchanged their life stories, she learned that he had been spastic since birth, and she told him of her terrible accident. When she brought a photo in one day to show him how she had looked before the accident, there were tears in his eyes.

Then one day he brought her joyful but frightening news. "Sybil, I hope you won't mind, but I went to see a friend of mine from college who is now a doctor. He said maybe your eye can be corrected."

Sybil, deeply touched, quickly interrupted. "Yes, I know," she said, "but when my parents were alive, they checked into it and found that the operation was so dangerous and expensive we couldn't think of it."

"Well, it's been a long time since then, and maybe your condition changed or maybe medicine has new procedures. You should check again."

After several weeks, Sybil went with Matt to see his friend. There was, in fact, a good chance for correction, but it was a long procedure and an expensive one. Sybil was entitled to some health benefits with her job, but she had nowhere near the money it would take.

With even more effort than usual Matt stammered out one day, "It's all set, Sybil. I've made arrangements for the operation and hospital stay. Don't worry about the money—I've used my mutual fund and borrowed the rest."

Sybil was operated on successfully, and while she was in the hospital Matt visited, read to her, bought her a radio, and kept her spirits up. A few months after she left the hospital, they announced their engagement. When Sybil's cousin Annie met Matt for the first time, she was horrified; she pulled Sybil aside at the first opportunity and said fiercely, "Sybil, you're beautiful, how can you think of marrying this man?"

Sybil answered just as fiercely, "He's the kindest man in the world, he's my best friend, and there's no one that I could love more than Matt."

Nurturing is one of the most important forms of wooing. Consider the story of Stanley and Connie. Stanley is a dentist in his mid-thirties. He's a bachelor, fairly attractive, competent, and solicitous of a patient's welfare. He is very intense about his work and had not given much thought to marriage because of his preoccupation with his practice. He had no great need to search for a wife because it seemed that every other patient was a potential bride or at least had a daughter, cousin, or best friend who would be perfect. He dated a lot and had his pick of the bouquet. Why should he rush into anything? The future stretched out to an unlimited horizon of dates and sexual adventures.

One day last spring he had a date with Connie. He had taken her out several times, and he liked her, at least as well as a half-dozen other women he had dated. She was attractive, intelligent, and fun to be with. But marriage—why would he want to get married?

It was her birthday, a Wednesday, and as a special treat, he had made reservations for dinner at the Four Seasons restaurant in New York City. She had told him she had always wanted to go there. That Wednesday, Stanley had a hard day at the office. There were several last-minute emergencies, and then his last patient fainted in the chair. Stanley finally brought the man around, but it was a very stressful event.

When Stanley arrived late to pick up Connie, she was waiting, dressed beautifully in a new dress, new shoes, new hairdo—ready for a gala evening.

After a quick hello, Stanley suggested they leave promptly to keep their dinner reservation. But Connie said, "Stanley, you look so beat. What happened?"

And Stanley told her about his day, conscious of how comforting it was that someone was really interested.

When he finished, Connie said, "That's it! We're staying home. I'll whip up something in the kitchen. I hope you don't mind pot luck or an omelet."

Stanley protested—it was her birthday! But Connie waved it all aside. She told him, "Give me your jacket, loosen your tie, sit here, and watch TV. I'll cancel our dinner reservation. We'll go some other time. It will take me about thirty minutes to make dinner for two at Connie's Eatery."

Stanley knew she meant it and was grateful. As he sat exhausted on the sofa and gazed at the TV, he could feel peace seeping into his weary bones. He thought about how nice it was to have someone who really cared about him, how long it had been since anyone was interested enough to ask, "What kind of a day did you have?" How good it was to have someone to share a hard day with.

Connie's nurturing and caring that evening was the catalyst. In the months that followed, Stanley and Connie both realized they were made for each other. A spring wedding is planned.

Let me tell you the story of our friend, Lillian. She is a writer, an attractive career woman, a chic dresser, quiet, and a feminist, the quintessential romantic dreamer. She's now happily married with three grown children. When asked about the catalyst in her marriage she told this story:

"I had reached what in those days was considered the very sobering age of thirty and decided that this was the year I would find and marry Mr. Right. There were a number of men to choose from, but there was a turning point that made one man different from all the others.

"David and I had met in Chicago and had gone out a few times. There was nothing special or exciting about him. He was older, not very glamorous, and came from a very different kind of culture than mine. His people were Latin, with strong family ties.

"That summer I went to the music festival at Interlochen for a weekend of fresh air and music. At the last concert, David and I ran into each other by accident and he invited me to ride back to the city in his car. I was delighted to avoid the long bus trip home.

"When he came to pick me up at the hotel, I was in a sweat, struggling to get my bags together and get out before checkout time. He immediately took over. He got everything packed, got it all together and stowed away in the car. He took care of the bellhop and 'tut-tutted' the desk clerk who wanted to charge me extra because I was a half-hour late in checking out. It gave me such a feeling of comfort. Here was a man who sensed my needs, who cared, and who handled the confusion beautifully. He just pitched in and helped. He was solicitous and protective, just what I needed.

"Everything about him improved for me after that incident. A short time later he asked me whether I would like to meet his mother. I was overjoyed!"

A nurturing nature is rarely included in our important criteria list. Yet for the long haul, it is one of the most important qualities for a happy union. Go back and add the criterion of nurturing to the list you made in the last chapter, and see if any of your leading candidates would qualify for a 3 in nurturing. If someone on your list deserves a 3 in this area, you are very fortunate in that friendship.

If you're not sure how to become a nurturer yourself, consider this rule of thumb: What would I really need if I were in my date's shoes today? Then offer it before she or he thinks of it or needs to ask. Offer it graciously and sincerely and really mean it. That's nurturing, the most priceless gift one human being can give to another.

16

The Turning Point

There comes a time in any relationship when it must go forward to reach a mutually desired goal, or it must end. The partners must find out whether they are on the same wavelength or not. The important thing is not to waste precious years in a dead-end relationship.

This is the tale of how one woman solved the problem of what to do when a relationship seemed stuck, like a flawed record with the needle caught in a groove. Teddy met Bill on a blind double date. In fact, he was with the other woman, but they gravitated to one another right away. And before the evening was over, they had made plans for their own date. Both in their late twenties, both plump and hearty in their love for good food and laughter, they soon became a couple. This went on for months, with no definite plans for the future. At last, Teddy unburdened herself. She reminded Bill that she was almost thirty, that she wanted to get married and have a family, and that although she really loved him, if they didn't have the same goals, they would have to stop seeing each other. Bill was shocked because he was perfectly satisfied with his way of life. He had no family to speak of, but he did have a group of bachelor friends who spent their spare time together bowling, playing poker, going to baseball games, and "just shooting the breeze." They were scornful when Bill told them of Teddy's ultimatum. Typical comments were "See, she's putting the squeeze on you"; "Once you tie the knot, you're sunk"; "Just like a woman, wants you to give up your freedom."

At first, Bill's reaction was "Yeah, who needs her? There's a million women out there." And for the next three weeks he went out with his buddies. There were the good old poker games, watching sports on television, and hanging around trying to decide what to do on Saturday night. But by the third week, Bill began to ask himself, "What am I doing here? This is boring— same old crowd, doing the same old things, making the same stupid remarks. I miss her."

During the fourth week, Bill called Teddy and asked her when she wanted to get married. They have been married for over thirty years and have two grown children. Once Bill was gone, the group of bachelors didn't last long. They all got married within the next two years.

Ultimatums May Backfire

Teddy's technique for creating a turning point doesn't work for everyone. If it's presented too soon, an ultimatum can terminate a budding relationship that might well have flowered into marriage. The timing must be tempered by your ability to perceive reality. If you think your relationship is very close and that you do indeed love each other to the point where you both are ready to forsake all others, then an ultimatum may be appropriate and will probably work. But if you have overestimated your lover's interest because of your own, it is doomed to failure.

If you're not sure, a series of small steps may give you the evidence you need to make a valid judgment. For example, suggest and do things that are concordant with marriage: meet each other's families, go away on vacation together, plan work so that you can spend more time together. Chip in and buy things for the home you both can use. Make new friends as a couple.

If the above activities and others like them work out, they can give you an idea as to when the time is ripe for a turning point.

When the answer is "I'm not ready yet, honey, please don't push me," follow your heart for a while, but don't check your brain at the door. Your future and your happiness should not be postponed forever because you are in love.

This advice is apt, too, when your lover promises to leave his or her terrible spouse or old lover for you but somehow hasn't gotten around to it yet.

Self-delusion can be destructive. One of the saddest cases is John, who is in his mid-thirties and who finally fell in love with a young woman in her early twenties. After five months, he suggested an engagement and a wedding date. She was appalled.

She was too young for marriage; besides, she hardly knew him. All this despite the fact that they had gone away together for a week's vacation and the families had met and enthusiastically approved.

John was at a loss because he couldn't believe she really meant it. He still can't bring himself to go out with other women. Perhaps she will change her mind as she realizes she misses him. But if she doesn't, bringing it to a head did them both a service. As it becomes clear to John that she really doesn't want to marry him, he'll be free to find someone who appreciates him and who does want to be his wife.

Turning Points Can Be Made to Happen

In a previous chapter, we talked about changing yourself. But can you change somebody else for the better? Can you help someone else come to a turning point? If you want to determine whether to go forward in a relationship, you may want to consider this question.

Conventional wisdom says that it's dangerous to go into a marriage thinking you'll be able to change your spouse. In my opinion, the observation that "a leopard can't change his spots" is a bit of defensive wisdom, a sort of warning that people will continue to act in a certain way and that they can't be changed. It is the kind of observation made by a friend or relative when you've found someone you're attracted to and who has some objectionable habits or traits.

I'm sure this truth has many applications, but change is what life is all about. Just as you can come to a turning point in your own life, you may be able to encourage and achieve major changes in others.

The story of Robert and Mary Ellen is a case in point. Robert was a highly eligible young man. Tall and good-looking, he dressed with flair and was an optometrist with an excellent practice. His reputation for being dull, however, was well deserved. For several years he dated almost every woman in town, and they were all attracted at first. But after a four-hour discussion of corneas, myopia, and contact lenses, their interest waned. They felt they were earning an eye doctor's degree in one night. After a while there were no more single women who would go out with him.

Then Mary Ellen came to town. She thought he was very attractive and was pleased when he asked her out. She was not unmindful of the fact that the date had more than its share of optometry, but when he asked her out again, she accepted. As their second date was turning into the same kind of dull evening, Mary Ellen began to get bored. However, unlike the other women in town, Mary Ellen asked herself, "Why?" Why does such a nice man, with so much going for him, drone away about nothing else but eyeglasses? He's intelligent, got good grades in all of his courses in school—why is he so dull?

After much thought, Mary Ellen arrived at a theory. Robert talked about his work so much because he was shy and insecure around women. In his field, he was the expert, and that's where he felt comfortable. When in the uncomfortable position of being with a woman who was not a patient, he held onto his expertise for dear life.

On the next date, Mary Ellen decided to change the subject before Robert got carried away with eyes again. Did he have any hobbies, she asked. She was surprised to learn that Robert's hobby was collecting hand-carved pipes. As he told her the history of some of the pipes and the people who gave them to him, his eyes sparkled, and he became positively eloquent. In this new light, Mary Ellen found him fascinating. He, in turn, had discovered another subject on which he felt secure.

As their relationship deepened, Mary Ellen kept probing for subjects Robert could feel comfortable with. She suggested a course in Chinese cooking that they both took and enjoyed. She helped form a literary club that met twice a month to discuss books. Robert, a conscientious and insightful reader, soon became the star of the group and led many of the discussions.

Just about the time they married, Mary Ellen thought to herself, "Why, he's the most interesting man I've ever known." All because of that third-date turning point when she changed the subject and dared to help Robert change. She succeeded beautifully.

Of course, if she hadn't accepted the second and third dates, she never would have known Robert's potential.

Mary Ellen and Robert's story points up the importance of another, less recognized aspect to sharing, that is, sharing knowledge. We are all curious. Learning about what's going on is interesting and stimulating, and we are attracted to people who satisfy this need. Alas, that's why so many people who seem to have every advantage are often perceived as uninteresting, dull, flat. They do not share anything that has interest for us, either because they are not communicative or because they really don't have anything to say. In either case, we tend to find them dull. That does not ipso facto mean that they *are* stupid or dull. It could also mean that *our* personal interests are so limited or narrow that we cannot find a mutual area of interest.

There is a message here for both ends of this equation. If you sense that somehow your dates find you dull, check whether you've failed to communicate or do indeed have little to say! If you're on the other end and you find that your dates are dull—even the ones who have a reputation for being interesting and fun—perhaps your ability to question your date and make the connections is what is wanting.

In either event, these are not hopeless conditions. If you suspect you may be perceived as dull, make a real effort to become more interesting. Develop a unique hobby or special area of knowledge and share your riches. You'll enjoy being an expert or authority on something different. On the other hand, if you find that your date seems to be from outer space because of things he or she wants to talk about, try to listen and find out why the subject is so interesting to him or her. Most hobbies are an acquired taste.

Making the Connections

There's a fascinating metaphor for the process of falling in love. Do you remember the old dot puzzle you used to do when you were a child? It often appeared in the comic pages. There would be a picture that was just a series of random, numbered dots with a caption that read: "Can you guess what's hidden in the picture? If you can't, connect the dots, starting with number 1."

Then, as you drew lines from dot to dot, the picture began to appear; and when the lines were all connected, the picture was finished. Frequently, you could recognize the figure before you completed all of the dots. And sometimes you'd know the picture when only a few dots were connected. The picture would just leap out at you.

So it is with finding a spouse to love. When you meet someone for the first time, how you feel about her or him is a big puzzle. There is a series of connections to be made. Then one connection makes the picture clear (like Robert's first discussion of his pipe hobby with Mary Ellen). This connection is the real turning point when a nice someone becomes *the* one. As more and more of the connections are made, it becomes clear that you are in love. The picture does not necessarily become clear to both of you at the same time. Have faith. Then for the rest of your lives together, you find new connections you never dreamed of, new connections that give you a deeper appreciation of the picture.

When to Stay Single

There are some single people who haven't been single long enough. Perhaps they've recently been in a bad marriage or are still grieving for a mate who has died. They need to take some time so that they'll be ready to make an appropriate choice of a lifetime partner and lover.

Jessica was a widow with two grown children. She was in her mid-fifties, but she was young in spirit, health, looks, and style. She was an excellent and devoted wife and very attentive to her husband during his bout with cancer. About a year after his death, she thought about dating. When I talked to her about it, she confided that her marriage had not been a completely happy one. She had gotten married too early; neither Jessica nor her husband had dated anyone seriously before they met. They were swept away by the idea of being grown up and on their own for the first time. The marriage had its moments, and the children were wonderful, but Jessica and her husband were never on the same intellectual or cultural level. He only wanted to watch football games and movies; she preferred the ballet and art museums. He was satisfied with beer; she liked only champagne.

Then she warned me: "If you ever think of setting up a blind date for me, remember this: He can't be over fifty-nine, and he must be a professional or at least a college graduate from a good school. He must be as intelligent as I am and interested in art, music, and literature. He should be very handsome and dignified, over six feet tall, with an athletic body, though I'd accept someone shorter if he were special. You may think I'm kidding, but I'm not! This time I'll only consider someone who is just right."

I was saddened. Jessica is a fine woman and had been a good wife and mother. But she's out of sync with the world. In her own way, she's an adolescent dreamer, totally unprepared for the realities of dating. She has created a dream man, and I'm afraid that's the only place she'll find him—in her dreams. "Too soon, too soon," I mused. "She hasn't been single long enough."

Jessica needs time to reach the turning point and grow out of her impossible fantasies so that she can accept the blessings of reality. Also, she probably needs a little time to be lonely, to appreciate the company of someone less than perfect. She's not ready yet.

Sandy was another woman who hadn't been single long enough. She grew up in a very religious household, and from the earliest time she can remember, she was conditioned by her mother and father to become a nun. She embraced this idea as a young girl, and after going through all of the required steps, she entered a convent.

The enthusiasm and high hopes stayed with her throughout her mid-twenties. She loved children and trained as a teacher specializing in kindergarten and preschoolers. But gradually she became unhappy. Among other things, she decided she wanted children of her own. So, at the age of thirty, she renounced her vows and withdrew from the order.

She got a job as a teacher. The first men she met were also teachers, decent, honest, and hardworking. Her gentleness and quiet charm attracted many friends, both men and women. Fortunately, her innocence and naivete frightened off several of the men early in her freedom. I say fortunately because Sandy had none of the experience or knowledge necessary to choose a life partner and father for her children. She was looking desperately for someone to marry and share a life. Some of the men she dated couldn't believe that her innocence was real and not an act. She was heartbroken in each case. Although she was thirty, Sandy had not been single long enough. She had missed the early explorations most adolescents go through as they begin to date in high school. The fact was, she didn't have the first clue as to what she really wanted or needed.

Gradually, she began to develop a clear image of

herself and set appropriate standards for what she wanted in a husband. It was then that she met Frank, a divorced professor who cherished her sweetness and integrity. They have been happily married for years, and she is grateful that she didn't choose too soon.

Another example is Morgan, who was married for twenty-seven years, with two grown children. For many years, he had struggled in a suffocating marriage and finally achieved a divorce. This wasn't the result of a whim or an infatuation with another woman but rather the continuous erosion and deterioration of his relationship with his wife. Their affection and respect for each other seemed to shrink with the family's economic growth. The bigger the house, the grander the social life, the less intimacy and friendship between them. Their life together was a series of squabbles, spats, and marriage counselors.

Morgan's complaint was that his wife didn't care about him. He couldn't talk to her about his needs; she always brushed him off and won every argument. She also used sex as a weapon, withholding it when he didn't do exactly what she wanted. Most devastating of all, she belittled him as a lover.

Her complaints were that he was too full of himself, that he never sought her opinion or views on important decisions concerning their family or money matters. She claimed there was nothing wrong with their marriage except that he was neurotic, lazy, and indeed a lousy lover.

Things got so bad that Morgan went into a mild depression, cut himself off from many friends, and spent his time puttering around the house and gaining weight.

Finally, they decided to divorce. There followed many discussions about how they would divide their assets. He always lost. Then one day he found a solution. Why settle up? He would give her everything! There would be nothing to fight about, and he could go free! That's what happened. She got almost everything, and he got all of his clothes, a piece of luggage, and peace!

Then the trauma of divorce set in. Morgan rented a room in a small boardinghouse with a shared bathroom. With great energy, he set about losing weight. He worked out and replaced his wardrobe. Many of his friends and acquaintances waited for "the other woman" to surface, but there was none. He had never cheated; all he wanted was a loving wife.

When he began to date, he was as timid and as insecure as an adolescent. But before long he found that it was getting easier, and there were all kinds of women for him to meet. His early standards were very rigid and almost hysterical: No women with children! No divorcées! This one was too young; that one had a bad family history. But as time passed and he met more women one-on-one, he softened his rigid standards.

In a few months he had taken out a dozen women, exchanged life stories with them, and was better able to put his own life in perspective. But he began to feel a desperate need to get something started. Every woman he met was immediately evaluated as a potential wife and replacement. Only those who might possibly qualify were taken out again. His friends told him he was too desperate, that he should take at least a year before making such a serious decision. They said his experience was too limited and his wounds too raw. He agreed with everyone, but within three months he confided in one friend that he didn't know how to act with one woman he had dated. This woman was one of his first dates after the divorce. She was a young divorcée named Kilarney with two children.

Kilarney worked, had a housekeeper, and was very sympathetic to Morgan and his unhappy marriage. They met happily and comfortably several times, and he was therefore thunderstruck when she told him after dinner one night that she had decided to stop seeing him. She had another boyfriend who was younger and who seemed to be more serious about marriage.

Morgan was crushed. During the next six weeks, as he nursed his grief, he came to believe that Kilarney was the perfect wife for him. Marriage and happiness seemed only a step away. If he had only met her before this other guy. Faint heart never won fair hand—he would fight for her!

So he took her out on a Friday and told her how much he had missed her and that he wanted to take her to dinner and to a Broadway show for which it was almost impossible to get tickets. He said he had made a special arrangement for these tickets and could take her any night the following week that she might be free. Well, she couldn't decide which night, but she said she'd call and let him know. He was happy; the extra effort had paid off. Alas, she didn't call on Monday or Tuesday or Wednesday. On Friday she left a message on his answering machine: She was very sorry; she had forgotten all about it. And would he please call her again?

Morgan was close to tears as he told his friends the sad tale. He was taken aback when one friend said,

"Morgan, you're a jerk! She told you there was another guy. Face it, she prefers him. Yes, she listened sympathetically to your story and also said to call her again. But don't you see? She doesn't want to lose you as her backup if this other guy doesn't pan out. You're in no position to make serious decisions. There's a kind of desperation in you to find a wife, and it seems to me you're picking another woman just like your last wife. Wake up!"

Morgan listened, but he was too hurt to let go. He set up an appointment to see Kilarney during the day and "get to the bottom of it." There was a happy ending. She confessed everything: "You're such a nice guy, Morgan, that I hated to let you go. But yesterday Michael asked me to marry him. I hope you'll come to the wedding—I have some lovely girlfriends I'd like you to meet."

The reason I say there was a happy ending is that it brought Morgan to his senses. When he told the story to his friend, he added, "You were right; I haven't been single long enough. I'm too anxious to find someone to love me. I'm not going to let myself get serious for at least a year."

"Great!" his friend said, but under his breath he added, "I only hope he falls into the right hands."

Whether you are a single "single," or single in the process of becoming a couple, there will come a point at which you must take some action to enhance the probability that you will reach your heart's desire. You must be sensitive to the reality of what is happening and strong enough to do something about it. Be brave enough to take a look right now, seize the turning point, and move ahead with courage.

17

Relationships

Recently I called a business associate in Vancover, Canada. He was not in, but his efficient secretary said she could probably reach him if it was important. I declined, and she made some reference to my last book. On impulse, I asked her if she was married. She seemed a bit startled, paused for a moment, then said, "Yes, sort of."

I told her the reason I asked was that I was doing research for this book. "I gather from your answer that you are in a relationship?"

"Yes, that's right."

"How long has it gone on?"

"Six years."

"That's too long! Why don't you get married? Don't you want to?"

"No, I'm perfectly happy. I have all the advantages of being married and none of the disadvantages. You know, I believe if it's not broke, don't fix it."

What a mistake! A relationship is not a marriage. It's a hybrid that is neither fish nor fowl and has the disadvantage of being fishy and potentially foul. At best, it's a testing experience that should lead either to marriage or disengagement within a year or so. A relationship—or living together as an intimate couple without the marriage contract—often works to the great disadvantage of one of the partners, usually the woman. (I do know of one case, however, where the man was completely distraught when the woman left him after a relationship of many years to marry another man.)

In a marriage, you have an open and fully disclosed contract of commitment: to love, honor, and cherish, in sickness and in health, until death do you part. Each of the parties undertakes this contract with the sanction and blessing of society. There are no ifs, ands, or buts that make this contract conditional on changes one or the other has to make or goals they have to achieve. There is no sense that either of the parties has one foot out the door, ready to take off at the slightest provocation or outside invitation.

No, there is a commitment surrounded by social and religious traditions and civil laws to make it binding and permanent. Where did these traditions and laws come from that has made the institution of marriage endure?

First, they come from religious faith. Almost all religions consider marriage sacred, something good and to be preserved.

Second, from society. This includes government, both federal and state, and the community in which we live. All are interested in stable, permanent, and fruitful marriages and have made laws and regulations that are designed to achieve those goals.

Third, from family and other people who are most important in your life. They want you to be happy, and in today's world, marriage, children, and the potential for a fulfilling career—in that order—seem to offer the best odds for happiness and fulfillment for both men and women.

What About Divorce?

Why are there are so many divorces? When people don't want to stay together, all of the laws and regulations in the world can't keep them together! People believe that's the great "advantage" of a relationship: Once you've made up your mind, you just walk and it's all over. Less fuss, no muss. Nobody has anything to say about it. It's completely private, just between you and your partner.

Yes, that's an advantage of sorts, but that is also the tragic flaw in the relationship.

Relationships as well as marriage are vulnerable to the weaknesses and vagaries of human nature, such as:

1. We're never completely satisfied.
2. We always want more.
3. We quickly tire of what entranced us only a short time ago.
4. We think the grass is greener on our neighbor's lawn.
5. We frustrate easily.
6. We get jealous.
7. We lust after our neighbor.

One or a combination of these human ills can goad a partner to the point where he or she says, "That's it,

I've had enough. I've got to end this intolerable partnership."

In a relationship it can be all over in two minutes. He or she just packs up and says *adios*. But not so in the marriage. You can have exactly the same set of events, the same provocation and the same impulse to call it all off. Ah, but there is a difference. Easy as divorce is these days, it still takes quite a bit of time and expense, both financial and emotional. There are many aspects to be considered and decided: the economics of divorce, custody of the children, the home, cars, insurance, pets, and so on. During the period before a final divorce is granted, there is a cooling off. Each of the parties has an opportunity to reflect on what caused this once-happy union to disintegrate. "Did I do something wrong? Is there some justification for the things he or she is complaining about? Could I make some changes in myself? Will he or she change?"

This cooling-off period also gives the couple a chance to see what it will be like after the marriage is finally terminated. In a separation, people experience being a single again, not a couple. This, of course, may seem very attractive when you're angry and still together. But the reality of being alone and on your own during the period of separation and predivorce proceedings can be very sobering. The opportunity to compromise and adjust to save the marriage may begin to look like a more reasonable option.

In my own experience, I have seen many reconciliations before the divorce became final, and I'm sure there are many more, even before a formal separation takes place. The parties can anticipate what the unhappy experience of a divorce entails. It's not that I'm against divorce per se; there are many times when it's the best solution. The tragedy arises when divorce is used instead of better options to achieve happiness for the couple.

After returning from military service as a young lawyer, I was rather biased against divorce. I was influenced, I believe, by the "Dear John" letters so prevalent during the war. Many a GI got a letter from the new wife he had left behind, advising him that she had met someone else, fallen in love, and now wanted a divorce so that she could get on with her life.

After the war, the people who came to me for a divorce were often individuals shocked and disappointed when they finally set up house together. Then they found out who they had really married in the surge of patriotism and romance or the desperate feeling that perhaps they'd never get another chance to marry.

I then believed in marriage almost as much as I do now, so I would do my best to bring about a reconciliation. I was very successful, and the couples would leave my office determined to give it another try. In fact, for my first five or six years in practice, I never filed a final divorce decree.

Then one day at a cocktail party hosted by friends, I overheard some people discussing divorce. One of them said, "If you want a divorce, don't go to that crazy lawyer Fisher. He'll talk you out of it. It happened to two of my friends. They finally had to go to another lawyer to get the divorce."

Today I don't think I would be so tough. Experience has taught me that "a mistake doesn't have to be a life sentence." Everyone makes mistakes. That's how we learn; it's part of the life experience. And there are so many reasons why you can make a mistake in choosing a lifelong friend and lover. When it becomes absolutely clear that you have made a mistake, why should you be denied another chance?

So you can see I do not think of marriage as a locked cell whose only key has been destroyed. When there are compelling reasons, a marriage should be broken.

The Advantages of Marriage

Nevertheless, the advantages of marriage over a relationship are overwhelming. Living together to see whether the experience is as good as the fantasy is like sampling the contents of a new food to see whether it's as good and wholesome as the description on the package. Testing is a reasonable and even persuasive proposal. But the sampling period should not go on for years. If one or both can't make up their minds after six months or a year, it should be good-bye and on to new horizons! When you're living with someone, you've taken yourself out of the market, so to speak, and reduced your chances to almost nil to meet someone else who might want to marry you. (If, however, you are still looking for or dating someone else during your relationship, you don't even have a real relationship. It's probably just sex or fear of being alone.)

Living together to try it out does not have the same commitment, the same solemnity, the same purpose as marriage and should not be confused with marriage any more than the pregame tennis warm-up is to be compared to the game itself. It has its purpose but should not be the goal.

I emphasize this point because I've seen very sad endings of relationships that have gone on for years. A few happy ones ended in marriage. Most of the others ended in bitterness and great anguish.

Family and Relationships

There are two other aspects to the relationship that create much sadness and anxiety: family and children.

"Family?" you're asking. "What has family to do with what goes on between two people in love? I can't let what my family thinks influence my judgment or action. I must do what's right for me. I'm an adult now, and nobody has the right to direct my life. What they say and what they think means nothing to me. I'll do what I want. I can do without the family."

Nonsense! You can never escape your family; it's part of you, just as you are part of it. When you fall in love with someone, believe me, you get their whole family: father, mother, grandparents, aunts, uncles, cousins, brothers, sisters, in-laws, ancestors—all of whom have had an impact on your loved one's life. Whether he or she knows it or not, each of these family members has created or produced some reaction in your beloved: feelings of affection or annoyance that you will inherit when you become a couple.

Marriage creates a joining of families. This isn't something new; it's been true for centuries. Historically, the joining of families was often more important than the couple's marriage. Witness all of the royal weddings where the bride and groom were selected more for the good of the family and their realm than that of the individuals. And consider the marriages that were really mergers of wealthy landowners or industrial or banking families.

Now, although you may not be a royal or an economic prince or princess, your family is vitally interested in who you marry. They may not like the person, but sooner or later they'll come around and accept the fact of your marriage. This will happen even in the extreme case, when you marry someone your family detests or someone outside their religion or nationality. It will happen even if you start out initially as banished from the family hearth. After you've been married a while and the marriage proves wholesome, especially if you have children, there is usually a rapprochement and a forgiving. The prodigal is once again accepted into the family fold.

In a relationship, however, the family just doesn't know what to do. It's not an open understanding. Theoretically, only the two principals know what's going on. Only they know what the conditions and commitment are. Family and friends don't like to talk about it. Should they be happy or upset? They sort of stand around with bated breath, waiting to see what will unfold and being careful not to rock the boat. Every family, of course, has an Aunt Harriet, who is absolutely scandalized: "I never heard of such goings on! What is the world coming to?" That's her contribution to solving the problem.

The others simply don't know how to act with the potential relative or potential scoundrel. Should your lover be invited to the family holidays and included in family affairs? Or should your significant other be kept at a distance in case he or she proves to be less than a stranger—an enemy of our beloved relative?

This condition prevails for both families, and so the tender couple in a relationship are rather cut off from the normal intermingling of their respective families. They may think that's great—just the two of them is enough! But they're wrong. "All we need is each other" becomes a hollow rallying point, as the reality of living will prove.

What About Children?

Children, the other source of anxiety and sadness in a relationship, don't show up as a problem at the beginning. However, one of the basic reasons for coupling is not to share the rent, the bed, and TV dinners but to create a family, to nurture, protect, and enjoy children. The love and joy derived from children and grandchildren is universal and one of the greatest experiences of life.

Relationships do not produce many children. It's easy to see why: children would create many problems. They would add stresses and strains to an already tenuous coupling. Children must be cared for, nursed, fed, clothed, baby-sat, supervised, trained, educated, loved, and supported, not just for a few hours or a few days but for twenty-four hours each day for many years. The prospect of such responsibility is daunting for many men and women who dread the thought of being locked into the role of parent. Even if this is the attitude of only one of the relationship partners, it answers the question for both of them. If the other insists on kids, there is the very real possibility that the relationship will be over.

There is also this risk even when the reluctant partner is won over. He or she may give in and say, "OK, sure, if you want a child so badly let's have one." However, the reality of having the child with all the attendant responsibilities may confirm the original fears and anxieties of the reluctant partner and end the relationship. Thus the other partner is left alone as a single parent with the child. Aside from the economics involved, which may or may not be adjustable, this makes for a very difficult situation.

In a marriage, children are a binding force, tending to keep the couple together, reflective of something they produced jointly. The couple has a continuing interest in the children's good and welfare. In a relationship, children pose a threat.

Now even if both parties in a relationship want children, it puts an unfair burden on the children themselves. Although the stigma of being born out of wedlock is not as great as it once was, society does still distinguish in many ways between children of wed and unwed parents. As the child grows up, he or she becomes aware that there is a difference and a hurdle to overcome. In addition, these children suffer more than anyone else from the deprivation of the extended family ties. They miss the normal intermingling with two sets of grandparents as well as aunts, uncles, cousins, and so on. They are deprived of the normal identification with both families, and often the families' religions and traditions as well.

Considering all of the above disadvantages of a

relationship, how do you account for their popularity? Well, relationships have their place. In the process of seeking wholesome, permanent coupling, a relationship may provide valuable practice. It does offer opportunities to find out about one another in greater depth than just two or three dates a week. But it should never be thought of as a sample of marriage. It's not the real thing.

Whatever other conditions you may place on or accept in your relationship, you should go into it for a finite time period. The relationship is not a life goal; it should lead to something: either marriage or the elimination of that person as a potential spouse. How much more is there to learn about each other after six months?

Yes, I know you can continue to discover things about yourself or your lover all your life, but surely you must know enough to say yes or no after six months of playing house. Face up to it, bite the bullet: talk or walk! Life is not a dress rehearsal. Just do it!

Now, getting married may not be the reason you entered into a relationship. The real reason may be to get even with your parents and family or ex-husband. What a loser! Revenge is such a bitter way to spend a life. The greatest victim is yourself. Move on. Give yourself a chance.

Many of the partners in relationships are unhappy, but they are afraid to do anything about it. If they insist on marriage, it may be all over, and what then? They may think half a loaf is better than none; it's better not to rock the boat. So you smile when they ask you and say, "I'm perfectly happy. If it's not broke, don't fix it." Baloney!

I truly believe that being in a relationship versus

marriage is like working as an office temporary compared to being a permanent employee. The temp sort of manages from day to day. She is free to take time off, work only as much as needed, and so on. But there are also many disadvantages as a temp. You have to prove yourself every day. There's always another temp who can fill your spot. You don't get most of the perks, no health insurance, no vacation buildup, no paid holidays, no pension. Why would you want to be a temporary when you could have a permanent commitment like marriage? Don't you deserve the most connected kind of love, forever after?

Epilogue:
After You're Married

After the honeymoon, it's a whole new ball game! Most singles think that marriage is a slight escalation from going together or just a more intense form of dating. Not at all! It's a new kind of relationship, and you have to work at it to see that it grows and flowers. Going together, living together, or being engaged is to marriage as a seed is to a plant. It is the precursor of what is to come. The seed contains everything necessary to become a strong, healthy, flowering plant. But it must be nurtured and tended.

It's wonderful that you are attracted to one another, that you enjoy being together, working together, playing together. This makes a strong foundation for building your life together. But a marriage is built brick by brick, shingle on shingle, with unique windows and lockable doors, his and her secrets, your favorite chair, and my side of the bed. All of these details and thousands of others must be worked out together. But don't be frightened or overwhelmed. It's easy; just make your decisions like friends. Marriage is a special kind of friendship, and the care and concern for a best friend's feelings smooths many a rough spot.

One of the strongest aspects of marriage is the realization, as the weeks turn into months and the months into years, that you hardly knew your spouse when you married. After marriage there comes so much more, such deeper understanding, such empathy and sharing, such intimacy and aspirations as you grow close with the years.

The very working out of the details of your daily life together is like the mortar for the bricks and the nails in the wooden frame. Each successful adjustment or agreement strengthens the odds that the next problem will be solved. The experience of facing family problems and solving them together is bonding. In time, you will acquire the comfortable feeling that your marriage is invincible. You will rarely think about it except on those special occasions when you smile and say to yourself, "How lucky I am, how happy I am."

A caution. So many singles think that marriage is a solution, like a happy ending in a novel or a movie. They go off on their honeymoon in a limousine, and everyone throws rice and calls out good wishes. The couple lives happily ever after. Alas, it is not the end. It is only the beginning, and it isn't that easy. Too often the couple fantasizes that marriage brings a new problem-free life. Don't be fooled. It's not a new life but rather an extension of your old one. For example, your family doesn't change or disappear. They're all there when you get back from the honeymoon. Your beloved must now be fitted into your galaxy of relations. What's more, *you* have acquired a whole new set of relatives, with their traditions, likes and dislikes, alliances and hostilities.

You may think this is a terrible thing to face, and you wonder: "Wouldn't it be better if we just moved to Los Angeles, just the two of us? We could see the family every few years when we go east for a vacation." Not at all. The family makes for the richness of your life. It preserves traditions, faith, loyalties, standards, and history. It also ensures your own family's future. As long as there's a family, there will be someone who cares about your children and grandchildren. The family provides a network interested in your happiness and welfare. Your marriage is important to them because it will either strengthen or weaken the family as a whole. So, consciously or unconsciously, they have a stake in it.

And, of course, this is true of your friends as well. You each have your old friends who were there for you before you met your spouse. You each have had a best friend, someone with whom you have shared your most intimate secrets.

Now there is an adjustment to make. How does your best friend fit in with your spouse? Whenever possible, give the old life a chance to survive the new marriage. It will help the marriage itself to survive. Don't reject or cut off the old friends. Remember, they were the supporting cast in your life. They were also an important part of your spouse's history.

Don't be jealous of your beloved's ties to friends. That loyalty only foreshadows the deepening closeness that will be yours in marriage. So don't begrudge her the long giggling telephone calls with her buddies. They are the lifeline with her old life, and they help her adjust to this new and strange relationship of marriage. So, too, you should accept his regular poker games or golf with his old friends. They were the oasis in the dry dull life he led before he met you.

Spending time with friends is crucial. It's a way of recharging batteries. After you're married, you will still enjoy all of the things that moved you toward marriage in the first place. However, you will develop a conviction that life shared with your one-and-only is a blessed experience. You haven't given up anything for love; in fact, now "you can have it all."